All Those In Favor

Rediscovering the Secrets
of Town Meeting and Community

D1637321

All Those In Favor:
REDISCOVERING THE SECRETS
OF TOWN MEETING AND COMMUNITY

Published by RavenMark, Inc.
ISBN 0-9713998-1-6

Printed by Queen City Printers, Inc.,
701 Pine Street, Burlington, Vermont 05402

*To order additional copies of this book,
send $9.95 plus $2.50 per book postage/handling
to the Vermont Institute for Government,
617 Comstock Road, Suite 5, Berlin, VT 05602-9194.
To inquire about municipal or non-profit pricing or bulk orders,
contact VIG at (802) 223-2389 or visit www.vtinstituteforgovt.org*

*To schedule a workshop with the authors
on Rediscovering the Secrets of Town Meeting and Community,
contact Susan Clark at (802) 223-5824 or sclark@sover.net*

RAVENMARK
138 MAIN STREET, MONTPELIER, VERMONT 05602

All Those In Favor

REDISCOVERING THE SECRETS
OF TOWN MEETING AND COMMUNITY

by Susan Clark & Frank Bryan

Foreword by Deborah Markowitz
Vermont Secretary of State

Table of Contents

Part I: Considering: Town Meeting and Democracy

Part II: Taking Action: Your Town, Your Meeting

Appendices

Acknowledgements

First, a special thank you to all of Vermont's local officials. We know how hard you work for your community. Mindful of the many hours you already contribute, we want you to know that this book is not intended to add to your workload, but to add inspiration to the important work you are already doing. And with any luck, it will enlist some helping hands.

When we say that this book can help Vermonters "rediscover the secrets" of town meeting and community, we know that the "secrets" are alive and well in many of Vermont's small towns – indeed, that's where we picked them up. By including a variety of them here, we hope that this small book can act as a creative catalyst. If we know anything about Vermont communities, it is that they can come up with a hundred great ideas for every one listed in this small manual.

This book is for everyone – the concerned citizen as well as the active local official; the newcomer to town meeting as well as those who have attended for years. It is no single person's "job" to get citizens interested in democracy, and no one person will succeed alone. We need everyone in this effort.

With that in mind, many additional thanks are in order.

This book is a not-for-profit enterprise published without royalties to the authors, and with the generous support of the Vermont Institute for Government. Accompanying workshops are funded in part by the Windham Foundation.

For ongoing advice and support, our deep appreciation goes to Paul Gillies, Deb Markowitz, and Mary Peabody.

Research for this book included many hours of interviews and correspondence. The kind cooperation of the local officials and volunteers we spoke with does not necessarily indicate any endorsement on their part of the views put forward by the authors. Our gratitude to those who have offered their time and wisdom to this effort, including:

Joyce Morin of Bakersfield; Paul Doton and Diane Rainey of Barnard; Shirley Brown, Hugh Tallman, and Myrna Tallman of Belvidere; Robert Gannett and Dart Everett of Brattleboro; Deb LaRiviere of Bolton; Anne Wilson and Yvette Brown of Craftsbury; Cami Elliott-Knaggs of Dummerston; Weston Cate and Jean Cate of East Montpelier; Bridget Collier, Valdine Hall, Tim Nisbitt and Mike Metcalf of Greensboro; Laura Sumner of Halifax (who will write her own book of town meeting stories someday); Richard Cassidy and Cora Baker of Highgate; Juli Lax and Allison Forest of Huntington; Gary Anderson and Carl Fortune of Hyde

Park; John Cushing of Milton; Joan Bicknell and Jim Newell of Newark; Deb Allen and Bob Greenough of North Hero; Patty Haskins of Pittsfield; Hazel Harrington of Pomfret; Colleen Haag of Shelburne; Shelby Coburn, Jim Condict, Kendall Mix, and Steve Wilbanks of Strafford; and Tony Lamb of Williston.

Thanks to our early project advisory committee, including John Cushing, Nicole Daigle, Bill Dalton, Kathy DeWolfe, Tony Dominick, Karen Ducharme, Jan Eastman, Jeff Francis, Marge Gaskins, Marie Griffin, Bill Haines, Steve Jeffrey, Juli Lax, Sam Lloyd, Martha Maksym, Jim Masland, Joyce Mazzucco, Scott McArdle, Edie Miller, Dancie Mitchell, David Rahr, Gregory Sanford, Chip Sawyer, Fred Schmidt, Dave Sharpe, Larissa Vigue, and Flo Young.

Thanks also for great ideas from Virginia Rasch, Kimberly Bushnell Mathewson, Linda Gionti, Peg Elmer, Cath Reynolds, Marshall Squier, Paul Bruhn, Ken Jones, Steven Glazer, Karen Horn, Robert Maccini, Marge Gaskins, Kate Rader, Terry Bouricius, Sally Schober, June Carmichael, and Kevin Dann. We are grateful for thoughtful review by Bill McKibben, Tom Slayton, Karen Horn, John McClaughry, Anthony Pollina, Michael Sherman, and Lola Aiken.

For wonderful design and communication skills combined with endless patience, many thanks to Linda Mirabile, Greg Popa and Rebecca Davison at Mirabile Design and RavenMark. Thanks also to Ruth Hare for long hours of talented editing and proofreading.

Hats off to the Middlesex Town Meeting Solutions Committee, past and present, for their efforts to improve local democracy, including: Russ Alger, Kelly Ault, Wilson Brett, Henrietta Jordan, Dave Lawrence, Tim Murphy, Nancy Reilly, Dave Shepard, Barb Whitchurch and Greg Whitchurch. Also, appreciation to Middlesex Selectboard members for their enthusiastic support of citizen participation: Peter Hood, Bill Callnan, Mary Just Skinner, Mary Hood Alexander, Walter Kelly, and Cindy Carlson.

From Frank, as is always the case on projects like this, a special thanks to Melissa for her help and understanding.

From Susan, many loving thanks to Mark Bushnell for wise advice, wise cracks, and constant support, and Harrison Bushnell for keeping everything in delightful perspective. Special gratitude for the inspiration of Delia Clark, who sprinkles the fairy dust of community building around the world, and Harry Clark – if social capital were counted in dollars, he was a millionaire philanthropist.

Foreword

The writer John Gardner once described March in Vermont as the unlocking season. As winter's grip weakens, the frozen landscape comes alive, from the sounds of running streams to the harvesting of running sap. Life did not really freeze during the winter months; it simply carried on in less visible ways. Thus it is with Vermont's democratic impulse. Throughout the year citizens attend public meetings, serve on boards, exercise their franchise, and cast a wary eye on the deliberations of their representatives in Montpelier. But the true, spectacular leafing of democracy occurs on the first Tuesday of March when Vermonters gather to discuss, amend, approve or reject the proposals that will shape their community for the coming year.

As Susan Clark and Frank Bryan note in the following pages, town meeting is much, much more than a symbolic exercise. It is here that citizens can actually legislate; it is here, like nowhere else, that we fully participate in government; and it is here that government is a practice and not just a concept.

Any observer of contemporary Vermont culture will tell you that town meeting is as important to our communities today as it was during the earliest days of our statehood. While it is undisputed that more people turn out when the voting is by Australian ballot – the quality of participation is different. When we meet face to face to discuss and debate issues and to share a meal, we change the quality of democracy in the community for all 365 days of the year. At traditional town meeting, we get to know neighbors whose lives may differ from ours, and whose interests may be at odds with our own. By listening to one another at town meeting, we build social ties that make it is easier for us to find common solutions to problems that might otherwise divide the town.

And yet, for all our celebration of town meeting, there is concern. Attendance is uneven, turnout lower than our rhetorical commitment suggests. The range of issues that we can directly act upon within our communities appears to be diminishing. Some municipalities are turning away from town meeting's most precious gifts – the right to participate in public dialogue, to learn from our neighbors, to not simply approve or reject, but to shape local legislation – in favor of the drive-by democracy of the Australian ballot, which limits "participation" to a simple yes or no.

It is interesting to contrast how we respond to threats to our two great March events – sugaring and town meeting. To improve syrup production, we have modernized equipment, studied the health of our sugarbush, and aggressively marketed Vermont maple syrup. We have created a Maple Research Center at our state university and formed organizations to educate about and support sugaring. We have expended state resources to meet threats from exotic insects, acid rain, unfair competition and adulterated products. As a result, Vermont continues to lead in maple sugar production and sugaring remains a key component of our agricultural and tourist economies.

And threats to town meeting? Too often we shrug and say that the world has changed. We are too busy. People cannot be forced to attend. The issues are too complex, or the results too small. That is why this book, *All Those In Favor*, is so important. Authors Susan Clark and Frank Bryan have created a valuable resource that is both engaging and informative. *All Those In Favor* doesn't just identify problems – it lays out concrete ideas for citizens and local officials who wish to revitalize their town meeting. From offering childcare and welcoming new residents to creating a Town Meeting Day holiday, Clark and Bryan's practical suggestions will improve Vermont's town meeting.

As Vermonters, we value civic responsibility, we cultivate self-reliance, and we cherish community life. The tradition of town meeting is at the very center of these values. Let us not give up on the promise of self-governance. Let us learn from our remarkable history and nurture our traditions so that we can leave town meeting as a democratic inheritance for our children.

Deborah Markowitz
Vermont Secretary of State
December 2004

"A meeting of the legal voters of each town shall be held annually on the first Tuesday of March for the election of officers and the transaction of other business. ..."
◆ Vermont Statutes Annotated, Title 17, Section 2640

"Each town in Vermont governs itself under the laws of the state. Every adult citizen is supposed to participate in Town Meeting. ... When the qualified citizens meet in the March meeting they are the legislative body, the sovereign, and the court for their town. By their deliberations and their votes the citizens determine the policies of the town for the coming year, and then instruct their duly elected officers to carry out the wishes of the town. The Town Meeting is thus an example of pure, as opposed to representative, democracy in action."
◆ Andrew Nuquist, *Town Government in Vermont*, 1964

A Town Meeting Invocation
(Danville, Vermont)

Let us bow our heads for a moment of silence and reflection.

(Pause)

We are gathered together in civil assembly.

We gather as a community, in the oldest sense of the word.

We gather to come together and try to make decisions;
about what is right, about what is wrong.

Let us advocate for our positions, but not at the expense of others.

Let us remember that there is an immense gap between
saying "I am right" and saying "I believe I am right."

And that our neighbors with whom we disagree are good people
"with hopes and dreams as true and as high as ours."

And let us always remember that, in the end, caring for each
other, in this community, is of far greater importance than
any difference we may have.

Amen.

*"We started doing this at town meeting when our local clergy
(and others) reached too great a level of discomfort
over church-and-state issues doing traditional invocations.
It has a quote from Sibelius' 'This is my Song,' and an echo
from the public service announcement our athletic director
reads before basketball games."*
◆ Toby Balivet, Danville town attorney and parliamentarian

Part I

CONSIDERING:

Town Meeting & Democracy

*"Democracy must begin at home,
and its home is the neighborly
community."*

◆ John Dewey, Vermonter,
and America's leading philosopher
of the 20th century

Chapter 1

THERE IS A TIME

*Town meeting is the true Congress,
the most respectable one ever assembled
in the United States.*

◆ Henry David Thoreau, *Reform Papers*, 1835

In many ways these are hopeful times for Vermont.

In many ways they are troubled times.

The same can be said for America and the world.

In our hearts, hope prevails. But hope without action withers into paralysis and (worse) resignation.

A call to action

This book, therefore, is a call to action.

Hope and action are rooted in connections: connections in space and time. From Bennington, Brighton, Burlington and Brattleboro to Baghdad – the four corners of Vermont to the four corners of the world – from Athens, Greece, in the year 500 B.C. to Athens, Vermont, in the year 2005 A.D. – the beginning of recorded time to our own time – a question has haunted the human race.

How can we live in peace?

In our beloved Vermont at the dawn of the post-modern era, we can help answer this question. And (like it or not) we *shall* help answer it, either by our action or by our inaction. Indeed, we are called upon to answer, for we are uniquely positioned to do so. Vermonters still practice (and practice most thoroughly) the planet's single best example of the single best way to live in peace. For us this way of resolving human problems humanely, this way of combining our natural and inescapable longings for *both* liberty and community, this way of common enterprise – this way of peace – is a way of *life*.

The world calls it democracy.

We call it town meeting.

In the spring of 2004 as this book was taking shape we were contacted by a woman responsible for working out democratic ways of governance in the mountains of Afghanistan. Could we help her arrange a visit to Vermont by a group of Afghan tribal leaders to watch how town meetings work?

"Of course," we said, but cautioned: "As you know, the conditions here are profoundly different, perhaps unimaginably different than in Afghanistan. We are very lucky in Vermont. No one threatens us. No foreign invaders have occupied us for over 200 years. We are remarkably affluent, in fact indescribably affluent in the eyes of most of the world's population. Our ancestors gave us democracy intact, bequeathed to us a full-blown operation, up and running. We have every advantage to understand and practice democracy here: education, spare time and, most of all, a society that teaches us democracy from our earliest recollections."

"Yes," she said. "But the fundamentals are the same. Afghans are people too! And the point is to give them a glimpse of how it could be. The point is to show them a living example of a real democracy. The point is to provide them not a ready-made democracy, but a sense of democratic hope. Proof that somewhere in the world local people come together and debate local matters, speak openly about them and then resolve the issue with a vote."

"On the other hand," we warned, "serious conflict often breaks out at town meetings. People get angry. Feelings are hurt. Besides, it takes a certain amount of preparation to understand how direct democracy works."

> *"Town Meeting is a way of life for us."*
> Hugh Tallman, Belvidere

The woman in Afghanistan chuckled. "Feelings are hurt? Well, at least no one is carrying an AK-47! Americans are so spoiled!" (She might have said, "And so smugly elitist.") "All we want is proof democracy exists somewhere. You must understand what it would mean for an Afghan woman to see another woman stand openly in public and engage in a political debate with a man or another woman over some matter important to her community. It's hope we are after here. And there is no better place to look for democratic hope than in your state."

The truth of her words may be difficult for us to accept. For we have long taken our opportunity to practice democracy for granted. And they remind us that all too often the most beautiful and important things in our lives are the most ignored. Her words also impart responsibility, and responsibility imparts burdens. Anticipation of these burdens may trigger a natural tendency to skepticism. "Why should we believe that Vermont leads the world in democracy? Maple syrup? Sure. Liberal politicians? Maybe. But democracy?

Yes, democracy.

All eyes on Vermont

In 1982, more than 150 Vermont town meetings had passed resolutions calling for a freeze on the development of nuclear bombs by the United States and the Soviet Union. This act caught the attention of the world. Preceding an address to the nation on the issue by President Ronald Reagan, PBS' Jim Lehrer interviewed then-U.S. Senator Dan Quayle (later to become vice president to George H.W. Bush). Lehrer asked Quayle: "You said it's not going to be the folks at town meeting who are going to resolve this thing, but isn't that what has happened? Isn't that the reason we're here tonight? Isn't that the reason the president's speaking on it tonight, because the people at town meetings raised the issue?" Quayle did not deny it, saying only that military experts would not pay attention to "some grass-roots caucus taking place in Vermont."

Why did the world pay attention to Vermont in 1982? It was clearly not because our citizens in their town meetings were experts on foreign affairs or nuclear weapons. It was because the world knows that town meetings are authentic, democratic governments and Vermont has the healthiest system of this kind of government anywhere. It was because in town meeting governments, no elected representatives intervene between the citizen and what the government says or how it acts.

In a Vermont town every citizen is a legislator. In a Vermont town the government truly is *by* and *of* the people. Town meetings are not public hearings, opinion polls or what Quayle derisively called "grass-roots caucuses." They are legislatures operated by ordinary citizens who don't leave their lawmaking to someone else.

The world listened to us because of the historic reservoir of respect and admiration it has for the way we govern ourselves. It listened to us because for generations we had routinely come together to buy ourselves trucks to fix our roads, decide whether to build a local library, set the salaries of local officials, vote face to face on kindergartens for our kids, leash laws for our pets, speed limits on our roads and street lights for our villages. It is because we do these things democratically *all* of the time that the world listens to us when we give it a bit of down-home advice on matters of global import.

The world trusts us because we trust ourselves.

As Henry David Thoreau said, town meetings truly are a "people's congress."

If this is so, why don't we cherish them more?

Paying attention to democracy

Town meetings are in decline in Vermont. We will not dwell on this. Beyond some brief documentation of this troublesome fact (to establish the parameters of the problem) and a bit of explanation of why this is happening (to better inform our optimism), we do not intend to emphasize the negatives. Hand wringing is boring and (worse) useless. We will curse the darkness only in moderation and spend our time in this book lighting as many candles as we can.

Still, it must be said and said with cold honesty: If we are to save our democracy, we must take action. That is the bad news. The good news is that town meeting is still remarkably healthy in many respects and in many places in Vermont.

We are therefore confronted with democracy's classic dilemma: how to instill a sense of urgency about problems before they get out of hand and when they are still fixable? How to plan to avert catastrophes when the storm clouds are on the horizon, rather than when they are upon us and the only action left is to dive for cover?

This problem is especially acute in matters of governance.

Consider this. As a society, Vermont makes a goodly effort to preserve things historical. There is money to save old barns, repair covered bridges, plan for the maintenance of scenic corridors and the like. As a society, we have been a national leader in taking bold and innovative steps to protect our physical environment. As a society, we spend vast amounts of effort and money taking stock of social needs and planning how to better meet them – in education, child care, assistance for the aged, medical protection for our citizens and so on. We have transportation plans and plans for our deer herd.

Why is it we have no plans for our democracy, the wellspring from which every communal action on these and many other fronts must flow and develop?

Vermonters understand the value of planning to preserve essential things. We have, for instance, (and we think most properly) insisted in law that those intent on developing Vermont's infrastructure of highways, housing and industry must first tell us what impact these changes will have on aspects of our common life that we hold dear.

We have environmental impact statements. Why don't we have democratic impact statements?

Without democratic governance, all hope for an economically sound, socially just and environmentally safe commonwealth will wither and die. We begin this little volume, therefore, with a call to pay more proactive attention to our democracy. For we believe that democratic governance is the heart of a good society. Vermont's history has shown that a society based on the town meeting tradition has the strongest heart of all.

"There is a time," it has been said, "for every purpose under heaven."

This is the time for Vermonters to take stock of their democracy.

Before it is too late.

Chapter 2

A STEADY PRESENCE

The importance of [the town meeting] must not be underrated
... the failure to grasp it and continue it – indeed to incorporate
it in both the federal and the state constitutions – was one
of the tragic oversights of post-revolutionary political development.
◆ Lewis Mumford, *The City in History*, 1961

Lewis Mumford's words (above) are instructive because in the 20th century he was one of the world's foremost students of the city and the metropolis. For him, the town meeting was a universal idea not limited to small towns in a very rural state like Vermont. He reminds us that history does not proceed in only one direction, and ideas about change and progress must be considered from many angles.

Town meeting: A tie that binds

We are liberals. We refuse to be locked into old patterns of behavior *simply* because they are old. We understand that the changing world demands appropriate responses. We respect change and the courage of the people who suggest it, whether in communities, landscapes or lifestyles. In this book you will be asked to change things.

We are conservatives. We refuse to believe that things need change only because they are old. We understand that many things that are old ought to be preserved and strengthened. We respect preservation and the courage of the people who suggest it, whether in institutions, art or ideas. In this book you will be asked to preserve things.

Most of all, you will be asked not to be bound by an inclination for either preservation or change, but to tackle the more difficult questions: What is fundamental and must be preserved, and what isn't fundamental and can be changed? What works and should be kept, and what doesn't and should not?

Still, this book is primarily about changes. But they are of a lesser order than the preservation they seek to enhance. Here is an example of what we mean. Many of us grew up under the tradition of having town meeting held during a "workday" on the first Tuesday in March. This tradition was formed when majorities of local populations were either farmers or worked to support an agricultural society (like storekeepers or lawyers). In dairy farming, March was a "down time"; cows are tended to seven days a week, so a Tuesday meeting was as easy as any other, and there was free time between morning and evening chores.

Question: Should we change the day and/or the time of town meeting to make it easier for people to attend? Pure conservatives would say no, why risk a change from something tried and true? Pure liberals would say yes, times have changed and so must institutions. Our response is this: Find out if a particular change would improve your town meeting without compromising its essential character, and, if it would, do it. If it would not, don't. Trust us: Both liberals and conservatives will find the answers more complicated than they may think.

Vermont needs to discuss the changes needed to preserve town meeting. But first we must deal briefly with what it is we seek to preserve, where it came from and what its problems are. Only in this way will we be able to deal intelligently with the means to preserve and strengthen it. We begin with our town meeting inheritance – our common heritage – and it is a goodly one.

> *"There are people who are willing to be fly-by voters. I don't think in that case you're a citizen – just voting is not enough. There should be intelligent voting, not just voting."*
>
> Weston Cate, East Montpelier

Thinking about change

When we think about the history of Vermont from our rock-ribbed landscape to the kinds of people who have lived here, it is difficult to name anything more resilient than our democratic instinct to practice real democracy – that is, face-to-face community decision making in the style of the Greeks of ancient Athens where the word "democracy" originated.

It took more than 100 centuries for nature to produce the land of primeval forests – populated for many generations by the first native Vermonters and then developed by Europeans beginning in about 1763.

It took but one century (1770-1870) for us to strip most of it clean. It took but one more (1870-1970) for us to abandon most of the land we had worked so hard to manicure into a remarkable maze of stone-walled homesteads and clustered villages. Our hillsides, first burned down for potash and cut down for lumber, then covered with sheep, then covered with cows, are becoming covered again – now with man-made "generations" of small trees and brush. In short, Vermont's landscape has been in dramatic and constant flux over the nearly two and a half centuries Europeans have been here.

Through all this, town meeting has remained a constant.

In the beginning, the newcomers were mostly English and mostly Protestants. Yet soon, Vermont had drawn an amazing array of religious sects and other groups practicing alternative lifestyles often shunned by other states. It began with Ethan Allen with his anti-Christian beliefs that horrified established New England Protestantism. But that was only the beginning. To Guilford came the Dorrilites. In Sharon, Joseph Smith was born and from him came the Mormons. In Woodstock, the "Pilgrims" held their property in common and adopted biblical lifestyles. In Hardwick were formed the "New Lights"; then came the Millerites, who later created the Seventh-day Adventist Church. Ferrisburg was home to Quakers, Putney to the infamous Perfectionists.

Throughout all this social ferment, town meeting remained a constant.

Moreover, Vermont has always had more ethnic diversity than most imagine. To the northern counties came the French Canadians, almost always representing from 10 to 20 percent of the state's population. To Barre came the Italians to quarry granite. To Fair Haven came the Welsh to work the slate mines. Towns in southwestern Vermont saw considerable Dutch settlement. In Ryegate and Crafts-bury and the surrounding towns of Caledonia and Orleans counties there is an enduring and self-conscious Scot settlement. Poles came to Bellows Falls, Swedes to Proctor, Russians to Springfield, Lithuanians to Arlington and Irish to Fairfield. A community of Rusyn-Carpathians arrived in Proctor to quarry marble, and in Brattleboro a Russian Orthodox Church had to be built to serve the arrivals from Minsk. Small in absolute terms but much larger in relative terms, these groups make clear that the assimilation of peoples of different tongues and ethnic backgrounds into Vermont society has always been a recurring process.

> *"The important thing about town meeting is that it brings people together to discuss things and listen to each other before they vote. We don't do that enough anymore, and we need to."*
>
> Lola Aiken, Montpelier

Throughout all this change, town meeting stood firm.

When first we came to Vermont, we came on foot. Pushing wheelbarrows. Leading milk cows. But within two generations, we had fashioned a complex pattern of roads over most of Vermont and we traveled by horse and wagon. Then came the railroads. They pushed into and through Vermont with amazing rapidity, changing where we lived, how we farmed, whom we loved. After them the automobile did the same, and now 64 percent of all Vermonters live in or adjacent to a town or city through which an interstate highway passes.

But town meeting held fast.

The first citizens of the new state of Vermont lived in log cabins, subsisted on food that changed only with the season, suffered through headaches and toothaches and died at an early age. They had callused hands – all of them, men, women and children. A light in the house after dark was a luxury. Today we live in a world and share a lifestyle that would be *unimaginable* to ordinary citizens attending their town meetings before the Civil War and even those attending their town meetings in the early part of the 20th century. Everything has changed so much.

Except for town meeting.

Vermonters of 1830 would be astonished traveling through today's Vermont to attend a town meeting. (Driving, for instance, in a heated car going 40 miles an hour over paved roads and listening to a radio – a radio! – while sipping hot coffee and eating a sticky bun.) But once inside the local school gym or town hall or fire station where the town meeting was held, once the moderator had called the meeting to order, once she had read the words: "The people of Craftsbury are warned to be at the Craftsbury Common School on Tuesday, the 4th of March 2004, at 9 in the forenoon to act on the following articles" these Vermonters of long ago would know precisely what to do. Town meeting would be perfectly familiar to them.

They would be home again.

Practicing real democracy.

Should we not shudder at the possibility that it might be our generation that let it slip away?

Chapter 3

A GOODLY HERITAGE

*Town meeting is the wisest invention ever devised
by the wit of man for the perfect exercise of self-government.*

◆ Thomas Jefferson, *Letter to Joseph C. Cabell*, 1816

What is town meeting? Where did it come from and how has it changed? Many new arrivals to the Green Mountains and, indeed, many longtime residents and even native-born Vermonters have questions about town meeting.

This is to be expected.

Taking democracy for granted

We know about our state government and (especially) the American national government from our earliest recollection – at home and at school. But local government and town meeting have not traditionally been important features of public school curricula. Attention to them has generally been limited to the innovative efforts of specific teachers. (This may now be changing, thanks to recent efforts by the Vermont Secretary of State's Office as well as other new programs.) Nor do we learn about town meeting in college. Post-secondary courses in local government are scarce and often limited to subjects like urban politics or county government. When survey courses are taught, town meeting is seldom given more than a passing glance.

Nor is this surprising. Until 2004, no book had ever been published about Vermont town meetings. Ever. Only one book had ever been published about town meeting anywhere, and that was limited to a short account of the legal forms town meetings take in New England and published in 1999.

Worse, national politicians, aided and abetted by the national media, have changed the very meaning of town meeting from a community *legislature* to a public meeting or (even more off the mark) to a political campaign technique. So-called town meetings turn up everywhere in America when people are called to a public venue to voice their opinions, hear a speech or meet a candidate. Television is full of "town meeting" debates, especially in election years. A recent study of college textbooks on American government and politics discovered that references to town meeting are as apt to be found in chapters on the media as they are in chapters on democracy and governance. It is a sad and ironic fact that now when more and more Americans are familiar with the words "town meeting," they know less and less about what it really is.

This underscores the most important reason so many people know so little about the essential character of a town meeting: Modern-day citizens have difficulty even conceiving of themselves as making the laws, rather than voting for someone else to do it for them.

Town meeting is a legislature, a policy-making institution. Every registered voter in a Vermont town that has a town meeting is a legislator. A town meeting government is a "no excuses" government. *You* are the government in a Vermont town.

To understand what this means, it is essential to know how it came to be.

Before there was an America there was town meeting

In the 1990s, the term "reinventing government" was often heard in reference to making the national political system work better. It was an apt phrase, because our national government was the most important invention ever created to govern a large nation. But our founders did not invent a democracy when they wrote our Constitution. In fact they feared democracy. James Madison himself once said that even if every citizen of Athens were a Socrates, the Athenian assembly would still have been a "mob." So they created a representative republic – and even there, only one of the two houses was elected by the people. Both the Senate and the president were appointed. Even today, the national government is (as, indeed, it must properly be) an approximation of democracy, using elected representatives to substitute for the real thing.

Besides, when the founders of our republic met in Philadelphia in 1787, New Englanders had already invented democracy. More accurately, they had *reinvented* it in New England, where it had been in full operation for more than a century. What New Englanders reinvented had originated 2,300 years earlier in Greece. It then fell off history's radar screen until we tried it again along the cold shores of the northern Atlantic. In these new democracies, American citizens (like the Greeks two millennia earlier) came together and made binding decisions as the legislature of a political union – a *government*.

And we still do.

Every citizen a legislator

What was unique about these New England democracies was not simply face-to-face decision making by organized groups of people. After all, this was already being done, for example (in religion) by members of a Congregational church or (in business) by a contractual entity like the Mayflower Company. But allowing all the voters of a *government* (in New England, the town) to come together and make binding decisions for themselves was dramatically new.

Those who settled a town often belonged to the same church, and often

TOWN MEETING AND "CIVIL" SOCIETY

Do we trust our neighbors? Do we lend a hand in community groups and participate in public affairs? Do we believe in equality and show tolerance for our differences? These are the kinds of things scientists examine when they measure "civil" society. And more importantly, they're what we all hope for the communities our kids will grow up in.

Happily, a number of studies allow Vermonters to make the remarkable claim that Vermont is among the most "civil" states in America. And it sure looks like town meeting helps. Five of the six New England states – *the only places in America where town meeting is fully practiced* – rank in the top 10 states for civil society. In study after study, Vermont often ranks first and consistently lands in the top three.

one of their first acts was to build a "meeting house" in which to worship. But wilderness survival soon trumped religious fervor. If you live in Bradford, your town deferred religious matters for 17 years, says historian Harold Haskins, "to keep body and soul together" and then deal with the "harsh years of the Revolutionary War." If you live in Waitsfield, your first town meeting was not held in a church or meetinghouse (there were seldom both in the early towns); it was held in General Benjamin Wait's barn.

In fact, church influence was more pragmatic than controlling. The town met in the church because that was the only public building. Early on, the selling of pews sometimes became a substitute for taxation. If you live in Wheelock, for instance, your historian Eleanor Jones Hutchinson points out that you once voted to require the town to pay for rum to be served at the auctioning of the church pews. She notes that when the town supplied rum at the auction, pews went for higher prices.

If you live in Weston, some of your fellow citizens once appealed for the building of a new meetinghouse as follows:

> How long, o ye, will ye dwell in your ceiled houses and this house lie waste. The Subscribers respectfully solicit their fellow citizens of Weston of *every* religious denomination to *cooperate* with them in what they deem a laudable object: the building of a meetinghouse for the *public worship of God and for Town Meetings.* (Emphasis our own)

Church influence was not only a source of cooperation, but of conflict as well – both of which are absolutely necessary for a healthy democracy. If you live in South Hero, you (like many other towns) once heatedly debated whether to recruit a "town" preacher. More than 200 years ago in 1793 you voted to hire Mr. Timothy Williams, "yea 47, nay 31."

SOCIAL CAPITAL: VERMONT IS "RICH" IN MORE WAYS THAN ONE

Some people call it neighborliness. Political scientists have a fancy name for it: "social capital" – that web of trust and connectedness that makes a town into a community. We invest in it whether we're chatting with a neighbor or pulling a stranger out of a snowbank, hanging out with friends at hunting camp or enjoying a book group. Or, attending a town meeting.

It's not just a feel-good concept. Social scientists can now measure cause and effect, and have discovered that having high social capital actually causes other concrete benefits. Communities with more social capital consequently have measurably healthier citizens. Their economies are more vibrant. And – get this – their democracies are stronger.

Studies show that Vermont is one of the richest states in social capital, and evidence strongly suggests that our town meeting culture helps us keep it that way.

So whether you want to increase or decrease your town budget this year, you'll be enriching your town by showing up at town meeting.

Conflict also occurred over the question of church (meetinghouse) location. In Bradford it took five years and many town meetings to decide on a location for a town-sponsored meetinghouse. In the end, the town voted to ask a committee from three other towns (one member each from Newbury, Vermont, and Haverhill and Piermont in New Hampshire) to recommend a site. They did, and it was accepted. Thus, outside consultants have a long history in Vermont!

If you live in Jericho, your minutes for the meeting of October 2, 1794 show you decided that everyone would "write his place for a meeting house and put it into a hat." You did. Several times. But you couldn't achieve consensus. Next you appointed a committee to come up with a recommendation to be presented at the next meeting. The committee met, and you rejected its findings a month later. To avoid further conflict, you brought in mediators from outside – from Williston, Essex and Burlington. Their recommendation was accepted. (Sound familiar?)

In short, our town meetings of long ago founded the principles of democratic practice that we know today. What is gloriously unique about New England (and especially Vermont) is that this principle of face-to-face rulemaking for exclusive membership groups (like a church) became

Executive and Legislative Branches What they mean at different levels of government		
	Executive	**Legislative**
National:	President	U.S. Congress
State:	Governor	State Legislature
City:	Mayor	Board of Aldermen
Town:	Selectboard	YOU – And all of your neighbors who attend town meeting

face-to-face *lawmaking* for a civil society – a community bounded by geography. And these laws were made face to face, in assemblies of the whole. What the Greeks had created more than 2,000 years earlier in the warm suns of the Mediterranean had been reinvented in the frost-bound forests of northern New England.

A foundation for civil society

From the framing of Vermont's Constitution (the world's first to outlaw slavery and provide for full manhood suffrage) to our ferocious and sustained hostility to slavery in the American South, from our leading role in the defeat of McCarthyism in the mid 20th century to our ground-breaking public debates on civil unions in the 1990s, from providing the world with its first ecologist in George Perkins Marsh to our national leadership in the modern environmental revolution with Act 250 – and the list could go on in so many areas of human achievement and enterprise – it is hard to name, pound-for-pound, a state that has given more richly debated, thoughtful social innovation to America than Vermont.

Indeed, at the turn of the 21st century, no state in America more consistently places better on indices of achievement in the areas of good government, civil society, social capital, collective generosity and political tolerance than our own state of Vermont.

It is important that every Vermonter know this.

It is also important for every Vermonter to understand that these remarkable contributions and rankings flow from our most crowning achievement, our town meeting democracy. It is no accident that the one historical constant and commonality in this homeland of ours is town meeting. It is no accident that the state that leads America in these measures of good government also leads America in the percentage of its citizens that practice face-to-face democracy as citizen legislators at town meeting.

We have demonstrated to the world that ordinary people can govern themselves. We have kept our town meetings. Surely it is this practice and this faith that have created and nourished the unique people we are, and the people we hope to continue to be.

Chapter 4

DEMOCRATIC POSSIBILITY, THEN AND NOW

[We] fight for liberty and win it with hard knocks.
[Our] children, brought up easy, let it slip away again, poor fools.
And their children are once more slaves.

◆ D. H. Lawrence

To understand the state of town meeting today, and how our heritage of face-to-face democracy may be translated into action for the here and now, one must appreciate the authority wielded by our early town meetings. The popular notion that "in the old days" government interfered very little in the lives of ordinary people is simply wrong. There was plenty of government "going on." The difference is almost all of it was local. Simply put, the towns did nearly everything. A thorough pondering of the difficulty of life in those times – of hardship almost unimaginable to the modern mind – compared with how thoroughly these people governed themselves begs a powerful, even haunting, question.

If they could do it, why can't we?

Reading the warnings of hundreds of early town meetings is like reading the agendas of hundreds of little republics where the citizenry was in charge – totally – of almost every matter of cooperative concern. In Guildhall's first meeting, they elected 12 officers, including "sealer of weights and measures," "hog reeve" and "fence viewer." They also: "Voted to raise forty Pounds Lawful money to make and mend highways," to "give six Shillings pr. man by day of highwaywork" and to "give three Shillings for one pair of Oxen per day on highwaywork." In one of Newfane's first meetings, they voted to "grant the sum of four pounds, silver money," to pay Luke Knowlton for a book he had acquired to register deeds. In April they voted to accept it as a gift.

In Bradford, the town elected two "overseers of the poor" at its first meeting in 1773. This prompted historian Harold W. Haskins to wonder: "The need for two overseers of the poor in that small community seems a little strange. In 1770 there are said to have been 30 families there. Three years later in 1773 there likely would not be more than 50 or so. By our standards today, weren't all of these settlers poor? What could most of the people spare for others? It is to their great credit that from the beginning they had the poor in mind and made provision for them."

In Wheelock, the first town meeting was held on the last Tuesday in March in 1794 at "10 o'clock forenoon." After filling 18 other offices with 12 citizens (a citizen-to-office ratio very close to what exists today), the town elected a committee "to lookout [survey] a Road through Said Town of Wheelock and to say where and on which Road Abraham Morrill [town clerk and a selectman] shall do the work that he is to do." Historian Eleanor Jones Hutchinson says (almost in passing), "Through the [early] years the routine business of town meeting was the election of town officers, the care of the roads, the provision for schooling, support of the poor and ill, etc. Education, welfare, health care, roads were routine in those days."

Democratic possibility

How many actually participated in Vermont's early town meetings? It is difficult to know for sure. Few towns have records that tell us. From those that do, and from a great deal of painstaking work by local historians, a rough estimate is attendance was seldom more than 50 people and sometimes fewer than 10. Perhaps 25 might be an average. These numbers represent close to 50 percent of the freemen (as eligible voters were called in those days), however, and in some towns probably nearly all attended. It is also known that meetings were often held several times a year in the early days. The first meeting in Jericho, for instance, took place on March 22, 1786, but five other meetings were held that year, the last on November 29.

> *"It's not healthy not to have discussion. Everything shouldn't just slide through."*
>
> Carl Fortune,
> Hyde Park moderator

While it is doubtful that there was ever a "golden era" of town meeting when nearly everyone turned out every year, attendance was much higher in the early days than today. Even well into the 20th century it was much higher than it is now. Given the difficulties of life (from hugely longer workdays and workweeks, to much poorer transportation systems, to remarkably greater potential for sickness and poor health generally), one is struck by how complete town meeting democracy was in the past.

This means that as we take a brief look at the state of our town meeting democracy today, we can be hopeful. The promise of our democratic past is that democracy works, and under conditions much more difficult for ordinary people than those we experience today. Those who believe that people are much busier today than they were in the past (and that includes most commentators on modern life) have an incomplete understanding of history.

What we really mean when we say we are busier today is that we have different priorities. But of this there is no doubt: our heritage of town meeting democracy was established by a people who committed vastly larger percentages of their spare time to government and politics than we do. Nor was life "simpler then," as we all like to believe. Its difficulties were as full and real as they are today. Putting a meal on the table, haying a field, getting rid of a headache, caring for the poor, finding a way to get your kids to school – all were more difficult and time consuming then.

Consider the little town of Craftsbury in the Northeast Kingdom as it was in 1840. So difficult was transportation over and through its rocky hillsides, it took 12 separate school districts to educate the children. The majority of the people farmed. They kept 333 horses, 1,718 cattle, 3,166 sheep and 658 swine. They produced 47,906 bushels of potatoes and 14,398 bushels of oats along with 5,705 bushels of other crops, 3,171 tons of hay and 35,412 pounds of sugar. Meanwhile they ran two gristmills, a hulling mill, two carding machine operations, 10 sawmills, two fulling mills, three carriage makers and one oil mill. Although the data are lost, there were almost certainly several blacksmiths and wheelwrights.

> *"I think people who attend town meeting really understand what the issues are. They understand it's not just the school board or the selectboard dictating – that they have a chance to have their voice heard."*
>
> Shirley Brown, Belvidere town clerk

Fewer than 1,200 women, men and children accomplished all this. And yet we think of their time as one of bucolic simplicity. If you've ever worked on a small farm or in the woods, you know that these people not only worked hard, they worked smart. Their lives were fully as complex and demanding, perhaps even more complex and demanding, as ours are today.

Let us rejoice in this understanding! For it opens great possibilities to us. One of the most glorious possibilities is this: If they can do it, we can do it. We have the time to do democracy ourselves! Governance is not too complicated! The question, therefore, is not can we practice town meeting democracy, but *will* we practice town meeting democracy? And that, truly, is a hopeful question.

Chapter 5

TOWN MEETING REPORT CARD

The town or the township with its primary assembly is best.
… The town meeting has been not only the source
but the school of democracy.

◆ Lord James Bryce, *The American Commonwealth*

Perhaps the best argument
for town meeting is a challenge:
Show us a better way.

Let's see how town meeting
stacks up when compared with
town meeting's alternative:
representative government. Let's
do a careful analysis and grade

ourselves in three ways. First, how does town meeting participation compare
with general election participation? Second, is there enough debate and
discussion at town meeting to make it worth the trouble? Third, how do
typically under-represented citizens fare under the town meeting system?

Attendance

Let's start with the numbers. Across Vermont, in an average year, about
one in five Vermonters attends town meeting. Or, more precisely: A study
of 1,435 town meetings held in 210 Vermont towns between 1970 and 1998
found that the average meeting had about 20.5 percent of the electorate
in attendance.

Let's look at that 20.5 percent figure to see what it means.

How does town meeting turnout compare with turnout for national elections in America?

Every four years, Americans have an opportunity to vote for the
president of the United States – arguably the most powerful person on the
planet. On that same day in November, they elect 435 members to the
House of Representatives in Washington, 33 United States senators,
numerous governors and many thousands of state officials. Voting is quick
and simple; on average, it takes 30 minutes to vote in this election. Consider
how much money is spent by candidates on publicity begging Americans to
go to the polls and how many groups emphasize participating in the voting
process for its own sake.

The turnout? On average across America, about 50 percent. Although 2004 was an exception, in an average presidential election, about half of Americans stay home.

By comparison:

- Vermonters spend almost nothing urging each other to go to our March town meetings.
- The average town meeting takes close to three and a half hours, using up most of a day or evening.
- Many people do not get Town Meeting Day off from work; attendance can cost people a day's pay. Evening meetings may mean the expense and hassle of getting a babysitter.
- Public deliberation – sitting in uncomfortable chairs for long periods of time, listening and debating – is more work than checking off a ballot.
- Plus there are psychic costs. As we have written elsewhere, "Last town meeting you ended up sitting next to someone who smelled like celery. If you have to listen to another impassioned plea for property tax relief, you'll go nuts. It is painful to see Jim, and he may be there. The Smiths will want to sit near you, and they are the most boring people you know." None of these is a possibility in the polling booth.

"Town meeting is the basis of our local democracy. You support it if you support democracy. And you hurt the democratic system if you don't."

Weston Cate, East Montpelier

Considering these factors, Vermont's 20.5 percent turnout at town meeting starts to look a lot better in comparison with America's 50 percent turnout for president.

And town meeting happens every year. Elections don't.

Keep in mind that we are comparing *annual* town meeting attendance with national elections that happen every four years. Thus, the 20 percent average town meeting attendance figure may end up being misleading. It hides the fact that, while most of the people (perhaps 80 percent) who go to town meeting in a given year were there the year before as well, many (perhaps 20 percent) were not. Those voters could be added to the tally of town meeting participants over the four-year period.

How does town meeting turnout compare with other states' local elections?

Comparing "local" to "local" is more fair, and here the findings are even more positive for town meeting. Across America, voter turnout in local elections for city council members, mayors, local bond issues and the like seldom exceeds 25 percent and is often dramatically lower – in the single digits. This shows that town meeting's 20.5 percent attendance figure is very strong, when you consider that attending town meeting takes a lot more time than dropping in a ballot.

How much time are Vermonters willing to commit to town meeting?

In the average community with a town meeting, Vermonters spend in the aggregate about 2,240 hours at town meetings taking care of local business during a typical four-year presidential election cycle. (And this doesn't count any special town meetings that may be held during the year.) In contrast, when we add up the time spent voting in the presidential election, off-year elections and primaries, the aggregate citizens of our typical town will give up 908 hours of their personal lives over four years. Vermonters commit nearly two and a half times as many hours to *governing themselves* at town meeting as they do to choosing others (from their local representative in the House of Representatives in Montpelier to the president of the United States) to *govern them*. Now, that's commitment.

> *"There are definitely axes being ground. But there are enough people being civil there, that the people who might fly off the handle don't."*
>
> Joan Bicknell,
> Newark town clerk

We may be tempted to abandon town meeting because we think it is too much work or takes too much time.

But Vermonters must understand: It is a delusion to believe that the easier, quicker alternative of voting for others to represent us would result in a significant increase in participation.

Speaking out

Attending town meeting is only a part of the story. The *quality* of town meeting participation far exceeds the quality of the voting act. In fact, it is so profoundly superior that the two are incomparable.

Town meeting's strength and richness resides in the opportunity to engage in the verbal deliberation essential to direct involvement in the legislative process. Town meeting is a *parliament* – that is, a "place for speaking." (And of course, the value of public debate is found as often in listening to one's fellow citizens as in speaking oneself.)

Citizens who attend town meeting use open discussion and debate to fashion law. As we review our town meeting report card, we ask the question: Is this opportunity for public talk dominated by the few or enjoyed by the many?

Once again the record is remarkably positive. In the average town meeting about 44 percent of those in attendance actually speak out. While it is clear that not everyone "has their say," as overly enthusiastic defenders of town meeting often claim, it is also clear that 44 percent is a very strong number indeed. We know this from experience. Community organizers, teachers, professional group mediators and others with large-group expertise are amazed to learn the degree to which the debate and discussion of a typical town meeting is spread out over the whole.

The broad, face-to-face involvement of town meeting is even more remarkable when the following items are considered.

- Town meeting is not a public hearing; it is a legislative session, featuring discussion. Thus, the moderator may allow participation by the same town officer or informed citizen several times. Clarity and judgment in lawmaking demand this. Indeed, in a town meeting, those who do participate average about four participations each.

- Studies show that speaking in public is one of our most dreaded fears, surpassing fear of heights, snakes, close places and even spiders. There is something about town meeting that helps allay this fear.

- Some of the time spent at town meeting is not discussion time. Voting by hand or by ballot, reading town reports, making community announcements and so on limit the time available for discussion.

Two final points are in order. First, intense public debate is often uncomfortable, especially when tempers flare. This happens far less than critics of town meeting think, however. Besides, there can be no democracy without conflict as long as people are different and issues are important. Isn't it nice that we Vermonters are not afraid to let our differences be worked out in the fresh air of democracy, instead of hiding them in the secret meetings of the few and the powerful?

Second, critics of town meeting often suggest that public discussion is controlled by a "hidden elite" that "orchestrates" citizens' comments pursuant to decisions it made the night before at some secret get-together. Poppycock. As Ralph Waldo Emerson put it, referring to a town meeting in Concord, Massachusetts: "… the rich gave counsel, but the poor also; and, moreover, the just and the unjust … every opinion had its utterance, every fact, every acre of land, every bushel of rye, its entire weight."

Also without foundation is the charge that public talk at town meeting is controlled by the rich and well-educated who have been trained in the skills of public speechmaking. This happens from time to time, to be sure. But the reverse is equally as prevalent. Robert Dahl of Yale University, one of America's leading scholars of politics and governance of the 20th century, reflected on his own experiences at town meeting in Connecticut in his book *On Democracy*: "As in Vermont, discussions in town meeting are not dominated by the educated and the affluent. Strong beliefs and a determination to have one's say are not by any means monopolized by a single socio-economic group."

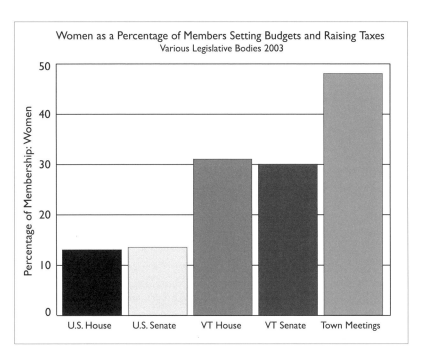

Women as a Percentage of Members Setting Budgets and Raising Taxes
Various Legislative Bodies 2003

Percentage of Membership: Women

U.S. House U.S. Senate VT House VT Senate Town Meetings

Women's involvement

How does town meeting perform when the task is to insure that typically under-represented groups are equally included in the process? The poor and uneducated aside, there are other groups in America and Vermont that have been excluded from positions of political leadership. Two of these groups involve race and gender. While Vermont (among the "whitest" states in America) has very few people of color, women make up half of the population. And in women's participation, town meeting has its finest record.

While laws made in Washington, D.C., or Montpelier or local ordinances made by city councils or selectboards are almost always crafted disproportionately by men, the record of town meetings (while still not perfect) is profoundly better.

Take a typical year in recent times – 2003, for example. Only 14 percent of the members of the Congress that fashioned and passed the American budget that year and raised the taxes to pay for it were women. In Montpelier, things were better. Thirty-one percent of the members of Vermont's House of Representatives and 30 percent of the members of the Vermont Senate that passed our state budget and set the tax rate to pay for it were women. But in a representative sample of 44 town meetings across the state in 2003, almost half (48 percent) of the citizens directly involved in the debate and discussion that led to the passage of the local budget and the setting of the tax rate to fund it were women.

If you lived in Belvidere or Bridport, Cambridge or Charlotte, Grafton or Lincoln, or Victory, Wells, Westford or Westminster, the *majority* of the members of the legislative body that approved the budget and raised the taxes to pay for it were women. The same can be said for nine other of the 44 towns studied that year. This has never been true in any (not one!) state legislative session or session of Congress in the entire history of the United States of America.

In Vermont, women *regularly* comprise a majority of the citizens who make the laws for their town.

We rest our case.

In short, whether it be time spent *at*, verbal participation *in* or women's share *of* town meeting, year in and year out town meeting continually outperforms other forms of the democratic process. There is more good news. Both verbal participation in town meeting discussion and debate, and women's share of town meeting attendance and discussion, are growing steadily and have been for some time.

But there is bad news as well. Attendance at town meeting, like voting at the polls all across America, is going down. Still, unlike the decline of voting in America – a decline hundreds of political scientists from coast to coast have difficulty explaining – the causes of declining attendance at town meeting are quite clear. Even better, we can do something about each and every one of them.

We turn now to that hopeful enterprise.

Chapter 6

PROBLEMS AND PROSPECTS: AUSTRALIAN BALLOT

Why do people come to town meeting? If they have a question,
they can get answers. They can change their mind
— or someone else's mind.

◆ Shelby Coburn, Strafford town clerk

We have seen that Vermont's town meeting tradition strengthens our communities and enriches our democratic decisions. Comparing town meeting with representative government in the United States, we know town meeting has dramatic advantages for ordinary citizens. Still, town meeting needs to be strengthened.

Now.

Here's why. First, an increasing number of towns are succumbing to pressure to adopt voting procedures that gut town meeting. Second, the population of Vermont towns has increased dramatically, weakening democratic participation. And finally, the actions citizens are allowed to take at their town meetings have been severely reduced from what they once were, reducing the incentive to attend.

Let's deal with these problems, beginning with the one that Vermonters can do the most about today.

The Australian ballot hurts town meeting

In a well-intentioned effort to include more people in decision making, an increasing number of Vermont towns are destroying their town meeting in the process.

The "Australian" ballot is a device that allows citizens to avoid town meeting altogether and vote on warned items on a simple "yes-no" basis. Under the Australian ballot, voters go to the polls, are checked off and use a pre-printed ballot to vote in a booth just as they do when they vote for the president of the United States. (The Australian ballot should not be confused with the "paper ballot," which is simply a vote during town meeting that is made on paper rather than by raising hands or saying aye/nay. A paper ballot may be used during town meeting whenever seven citizens request it.)

In the beginning, the Australian ballot was used for the election of officers only, and most larger towns now use it for this purpose.

In recent years, however, we are seeing a growing trend to put the town and/or school budget (and sometimes all spending items) on an Australian ballot. A few towns have placed all the warning items on a ballot.

Voting by Australian ballot is much simpler than going to town meeting. It is much less time consuming. It is much less public, done alone behind curtains. It is much less threatening—no one ever knows what you think. The Australian ballot is quick, easy, private, unaccountable and, most important, simple.

It is also deadly.

In a way, the Australian ballot is worse than deadly, because it doesn't kill town meeting quickly. And the execution is dishonest. We are told it will save town meeting, while the reality is that it poisons it and lets it die slowly, sparing the executioner the moment of death and the acceptance of responsibility.

> *"With Australian ballot, you won't be able to amend the budget. You can only vote yes or no. Yes, no, yes, no. It's the most inarticulate conversation you'll ever have."*
>
> Paul Gillies, former Vermont deputy secretary of state

Understand. The Australian ballot takes away your right to *legislate* – to be part of the lawmaking process – and it doesn't even replace it with a deliberative body that represents you. It simply allows you to vote up or down, yes or no, on an issue prepared by the selectboard or in many cases by a small group of private citizens with a special interest.

In short, it leaves the town with neither a legislature nor a town meeting. In doing so, it compromises the actions of the selectboard or school board, which must anticipate how the community will react to an issue and then submit this best guess to a winner-take-all decision.

By removing the option of amendment, flexibility is forfeited. The right to deliberate, compromise and amend is lost. School boards watch as entire budgets go down because a simple compromise on one issue is impossible. Selectboards see important community projects scuttled because they have misread the mood of the community – projects defeated that could have been saved at a town meeting with a simple nip or tuck from the floor.

Using the Australian ballot instead of a town meeting is like creating an ice sculpture by taking one great swing at a block of ice with a sledgehammer instead of carefully applying a chisel with care over time.

Advocates of Australian ballot argue that an "informational meeting" the night before fills the void, but in practice these meetings are no substitute

PEACHAM SAVES ITS TOWN MEETING

On a cold night in mid-December, the voters of Peacham debated whether to adopt the Australian ballot for their town and school meeting. In the discussion, Robert Maccini offered these words:

"We've been hearing the argument that even if the number of people who can't attend town meeting is small, those few people still are denied their right to vote, and that is unacceptable in a democracy. This argument is wrong because it fundamentally misunderstands what a town meeting is. If town meeting really denied people the right to vote, it would have been outlawed a long time ago, but instead it is widely admired as the last bastion of true democracy in the face of bloated big government.

"There's a legitimate reason why town meeting requires us to be present to vote, and it's this: Town meeting is not a ballot box or a voting booth, and it's not a state or federal election; town meeting is a body of citizen lawmakers, a local legislature, and every one of us is a legislator. Like any other legislature, its members must be present to participate and vote, and like any other legislature, it can, should and must meet even if some of its members are absent."

By a vote of 146 to 53, Peacham rejected the Australian ballot.

for town meeting decision making. Informational meetings are almost always poorly attended. Vermonters don't simply want to be heard; they want to act. Research shows that Vermonters are much more likely to make time for meetings when actual decisions will be made there.

Does traditional town meeting exclude citizens who would otherwise participate? And if so, does Australian ballot solve this problem?

These are important considerations, and they must be met head on. To do this we offer the following:

- With the Australian ballot, many more people will participate, it is argued. But how many more? This "quicker, easier, simpler" way of participating is not all it's cracked up to be. In Vermont towns, Australian ballot turnout seldom exceeds 40 percent and most often is under 30 percent. Most of these are citizens who go to town meeting anyway. This is evidence that town meeting does not deny participation to large numbers of people *who would otherwise participate*.

- Across the country, voter turnout in local elections (using printed ballots) is rarely higher than 25 percent, and is usually much lower.

While Vermont towns that trade town meeting for Australian balloting may increase voter turnout in the short run (if only by a little bit), we have to wonder: What about the long run? States with no town meeting culture – as Vermont is threatening to become – lack the advantages of our face-to-face deliberation and yet often get lower turnout in local elections than we currently see with our traditional town meetings.

- In general, town meetings held at night, when most people are not at work, produce attendance no higher than town meetings held right in the middle of the workday. Likewise, no evidence exists that attendance is generally higher at a Saturday town meeting than it is on Tuesday. These are telling facts, because they demonstrate that it is not work and the economic considerations that go with work that keep people from participation, but rather our priorities in allocating our spare time.

- Still, some people can't go to town meeting – perhaps they can't take time off from work or are away in the military or are homebound. Should we give up on town meeting because of them? If this were a significant and constant number, we would say yes. But it is a tiny number. Again we stress: Town meeting is not a polling booth. It is a legislature. And in a Vermont town, citizens, as legislators, need to be present to take part.

- Finally, there are other things we should do to reduce the number who "can't attend" town meeting to almost nothing. Most importantly, we must make sure everyone who wants to get time off for town meeting can do so. (See "A Day for Democracy," p. 70.)

Town meeting attendance (except in the smaller towns) will almost always be somewhat lower than voting booth attendance. However, as long as there is no important systematic bias against certain groups of people, changing to a ballot system and ending town meeting would be a tragedy. As long as participation remains a viable choice for citizens, a small deficit in the *quantity* of participation should not be used as a reason to destroy the magnificent surplus in the *quality* of participation town meeting offers:

- Face-to-face participation teaches forbearance and tolerance. It teaches respect for others' views. It teaches citizenship.

- Town meeting allows citizens to hear "both sides of the story." It builds an appreciation for the complications often involved in the simplest policies.

- By allowing citizens actually to fashion the law themselves, it creates a sense of "ownership" of the town's business not present when decisions are made by others.

- Town meeting is more efficient. Allowing citizens the right to change town budgets from the floor often satisfies objections and avoids the

WHEN SOME CANNOT ATTEND

Those Vermonters in the military who are stationed overseas at town meeting time will not be able to vote in their town meetings. Some might say this is an argument to switch to Australian ballot (so that absentee ballots can be issued). Major General Martha Rainville doesn't agree. She supports maintaining the face-to-face town meeting tradition.

She said, "Today's Green Mountain Boy must sometimes temporarily relinquish the ability to participate in town meeting due to the obligations of their freely accepted military duty. This is a small price of service.

"Town Meeting Day and the Green Mountain Boys are unique institutions in Vermont. The independent spirit of the 'Boys' leads us to try harder, perform to a higher standard, and to never accept the status quo. This spirit is also present at town meeting as we express our opinions and participate in the democratic process. The result of this spirit in both institutions is government by the people and for the people, just as our forefathers intended."

Major General Martha Rainville is the Adjutant General in command of the Vermont National Guard.

time-consuming process of re-voting a budget again and again, which often happens with the Australian ballot system.

- Town meetings build community by bringing people together. Yes, from time to time difficult personalities will hold the floor. Yes, conflict often occurs – and it should. But when successfully resolved in an open and honest manner, wounds heal more quickly and leave the body politic stronger than ever.

- Town meetings strengthen civil society in the larger political communities of which they are a part. There is a clear correlation between a state's use of traditional town meetings and stronger democracy at the state level.

- Unlike the polling booth, town meetings can be exciting, interesting and fun. They bring politics to *life*. Here laughter is often heard. Here we meet neighbors we haven't seen for ages. Here we learn that "Bill Stone over on the North Road is having trouble in mud season too." Here we discover that the town library is offering a new program for our kids. Here, most of all, we get to see ourselves in the full light of real democracy. Here, for one shining moment, we can be a Socrates.

- Like we said. It can be fun. Good fun.

Chapter 7

PROBLEMS AND PROSPECTS:
A QUESTION OF SIZE

*As we get bigger, people are relying more on government to solve
all their problems. And it's scary, because that won't work.
We need people to participate.*

◆ John Cushing, Milton town clerk

Vermont's small-town way of life is one of the things
we hold most dear. And yet towns continue to grow.
The price we pay is nowhere more costly than for local
democracy – our town meetings.

Town meetings work better, dramatically better, in
towns with small populations than in towns with big
populations. Towns like Waltham, Grafton, Sandgate, Belvidere, Roxbury
and Wheelock (all with fewer than 600 voters on the checklist) average
30 percent attendance at town meeting, while towns like Middlebury,
Bennington, Hartford, Waterbury and Swanton (all with more than
3,600 voters on the checklist) average about 5 percent.

Analysis shows that increasing town size accounts for much of the
decline in attendance at town meeting we have seen since 1970. The logic is
clear. In a small town, your presence at town meeting counts for much more
than it does in larger towns. Also, small-town people feel more responsibility
to participate: Since their lives as citizens are more visible, they are better
connected with each other, and they feel more needed by the community.

Beyond taking steps to control community growth, how can we deal with
this problem? The first thing we must do is to recognize that it is a problem.
Even the most ardent supporters of town meeting must face the fact that,
while town meetings are enormously effective in the smaller towns they were
designed for, they have not proven effective when populations grow beyond
a certain point. We are asking town meetings to perform an impossible task.
When they fail at this task, critics use this failure to undermine the very idea
of town meeting.

It is time to roll up our sleeves and figure out how to preserve the best
elements of town meeting democracy in larger communities. Therefore, in
places that have outgrown the practical capacity for traditional town meeting
(and we think communities with populations of over 5,000 are approaching
this point), we offer the following alternatives.

(1) Consider a new charter that provides for a city form of government (mayor and city council) for major city-wide issues, while creating smaller divisions where "neighborhood meetings" (with the full force of town meetings) have control over more localized matters. Indeed, this plan has been considered and is perfectly appropriate for a large city like Burlington.

The Vermont village tradition has some lessons to offer here. When geographic size of the town suggested it, villages were created, legally incorporated and empowered to perform functions appropriate to their needs, such as lighting and plowing the streets. The functions of "neighborhood meeting" governments within cities would undoubtedly be different. But the scope of public services has increased dramatically everywhere, and there are many "city" functions in place now – such as early child care, neighborhood youth centers, elder care, and neighborhood schools – that could be performed more efficiently at the neighborhood level. In this way, all Vermonters (not just small-town dwellers) could share in the experience of being lawmakers with binding decision-making power on important matters directly affecting their lives.

(2) Adopt the representative town meeting system. Here, town meeting "members" are elected at large from a small number of districts and go to town meeting to represent the citizens of their neighborhoods.

This kind of system has the advantage of preserving a face-to-face town meeting run by real citizens in exactly the format used by traditional town meetings. Suppose a town with 10,000 voters elects 200 citizens to attend town meeting. The system's disadvantage (that all the citizens are not legislators all the time) is mitigated by the fact that any citizen with an inclination to be a legislator can easily become one. Thus, the representative town meeting dramatically enhances "representation" (each elected member stands in for only 50 voters) and real democracy (any citizen may easily become a town meeting member).

Brattleboro, the only Vermont town to use representative town meeting, adopted this system in the late 1950s. In Massachusetts, more than 40 towns and cities have adopted this form of government. They may not be "real" town meetings, but they are the next-best thing. More importantly, for very large towns and small cities, they *are* the best thing.

At what point should a town consider shifting away from town meeting and adopting either the neighborhood meeting or representative town meeting? A few facts:

- In Massachusetts, the state constitution prescribes that a town must have at least 6,000 inhabitants before it may adopt a representative town meeting. Many towns with more than 20,000 people, including Plymouth with 88,000, use representative town meeting.
- Here in Vermont we find that when a town's population exceeds 5,000, it almost never turns out 10 percent of its registered voters to town meeting. Indeed, the turnout averages between 5 and 7 percent.

In addition, as the number of citizens in the meeting place increases, the percentage who have a chance to speak decreases.

Considering all this, can we recommend a clear "breaking point" population for town meeting? We can, but we won't. That question is up to the citizens of each town to answer. Given the data on size, attendance and participation, however, we make the following suggestions:

- If **towns or villages** reach populations of more than 5,000, they may want to consider the representative town meeting. But they should use caution, because town meetings *can* work well in towns of this size. Communities in this category include:

Essex Junction	St. Johnsbury	Middlebury	Shelburne
Milton	Springfield	Northfield	Swanton
St. Albans Town	Williston		

- **Cities** (which do not use town meetings in Vermont) with populations of more than 5,000 but fewer than 20,000 should definitely consider moving up to a representative town meeting system. Examples include:

Barre City	St. Albans City	Montpelier	S. Burlington
Newport City	Winooski	Rutland City	

- **Towns** with populations of more than 10,000 should definitely consider using the representative town meeting system. Examples include:

Bennington	Colchester	Hartford

Other opportunities

(1) Towns like Jericho, Lyndon and Rockingham, which have a bit more than 5,000 population but also have incorporated villages within their borders, might well keep their town meetings because their villages have "town" meetings as well.

(2) Vergennes is small enough to move from a city up to a traditional town meeting.

(3) Essex Town and Essex Junction or Northfield Town and Northfield Village might consider a representative town meeting to facilitate a consolidation, which has often been considered in these communities.

(4) Burlington is not too big for a representative town meeting, but it might also want to consider instituting several "neighborhood meeting" governments within the city.

Any town considering these types of fundamental change could also take this opportunity to examine methods for more representative elections. Innovative proportional or semi-proportional voting systems exist where voters can rank their choices or otherwise weight their support for various candidates. This can result in more equitable representation for minority groups. Towns could even consider using the ancient Greek method (still used in the United States for jury selection) of choosing representatives to town meeting by lottery among all willing residents.

HOW DOES BRATTLEBORO'S REPRESENTATIVE TOWN MEETING WORK?

Every Town Meeting Day, the people of Brattleboro go to the polls and elect a number of town meeting members to stand in for them at Brattleboro's annual town meeting, which is held the third Saturday after Town Meeting Day.

The citizens of Brattleboro elect these members from the three districts that serve as the basis for the election of their state representatives. Each citizen elected serves a three-year term. Since each district holds about 3,000 voters and each district sends 45 members to town meeting, the ratio of citizens to members is about 65-to-1.

When one considers that the ratio for our representatives in Montpelier is about 2,800-to-1 and the ratio for our representative in Congress is about 420,000-to-1, the Brattleboro "town meeting" is far closer to a real town meeting than it is to representative democracy. Moreover, the size of the deliberative body at each town meeting in Brattleboro (148 citizens – the 135 elected members, plus five school board members, five selectboard members, and three state representatives) is remarkably close to the size of the average town meeting in Vermont.

Other facts about Brattleboro's representative town meeting:

• Any citizen of the town may attend and speak, but only elected members may vote.

• Members of the school board and selectboard are voting members of the town meeting.

• Nothing is final for five days after the town meeting. In that time, if a petition has been presented for a re-vote on any of the articles passed at town meeting, a re-vote must be held.

• Those elected to the representative town meeting are called members and not representatives, thus emphasizing the notion that the intent is to create by election a virtual (if downsized) re-creation of the community, rather than a representative body as such.

Chapter 8

PROBLEMS AND PROSPECTS: ISSUES MATTER

You cannot run away from a weakness. You must some time fight it out or perish. And if that be so, why not now? And where you stand?
◆ Robert Louis Stevenson

We now come to the third of the three most difficult quandaries regarding town meeting: the question of what issues we have the power to address at the local level. Except for town size, issues are the single most important factor that draws Vermonters to town meeting.

Many people believe that we attend town meeting primarily for social, not politcal, reasons. But studies show definitively that the reverse is true. Social factors are important and reinforcing. But town meeting attendance is highest, and democracy works best, when important issues are at stake. Yale's Robert Dahl wrote in his recent book, *On Democracy,* "When citizens know that the issues to be dealt with are trivial or uncontroversial, they choose to stay home – and why not? But controversial issues bring them out." In the early 1970s, a young political scientist from the Massachusetts Institute of Technology came to Vermont to study town meeting. Her resulting book, *Beyond Adversary Democracy,* became a classic, and Jane Mansbridge was well on her way to becoming one of America's most important democratic theorists. Her treatment of town meeting remains the single best treatment of real democracy in a single town ever published. Here is what Mansbridge said about the loss of decision-making authority at town meeting:

> [As Rousseau said] … people are not likely to "fly to the assemblies" when the decisions they make in these assemblies are trivial … *it is remarkable that attendance at town meeting is as strong as it is, given the extent to which the towns have lost power to decide on important matters."* (Emphasis our own)

As we have discussed, Vermont's earliest town meeting attendees dealt directly with the most fundamental issues of human society – from building the community's infrastructure to educating children to caring for the poor

A WORD ABOUT SCHOOLS AND COMMUNITY

There is no institution in a civil society as important as its schools. A community without a school is a bare and fragile thing.

The best-attended town meetings are therefore those that combine school and town meetings on the same day. Total attendance at town meetings held without school issues at stake is lower than when school issues are present. Worse, total attendance at meetings when only school issues are decided is dramatically lower. Finally, when school meetings are separated from town meetings *and* the Australian ballot is employed to decide the budget, the result can be horrendous for meeting attendance. (And those who generally support school budgets should also remember that this formula increases the likelihood of defeat.)

Historically, when the practice of separating school and town meetings began, many school officials naturally had the best interest of the educational system at heart. This would be good for education, they reasoned, because only those most interested in education would attend, and they would be more supportive of educational policies.

This logic was seriously flawed. Taking democratic politics out of policy formation in any area transforms that interest from a *public* interest into a *special* interest. Wise educational leaders know that when parents alone support public education, public education is doomed. Those who work in the school system and the parents most interested in their children's education make up the huge majority of those who attend school meetings held separately from town meetings. This is a disaster for democratic education, for the huge majority of those who pay the taxes that support the schools fall into neither group.

The future of public education depends on communities full of people who are willing to pay for good education – with their time, their wisdom and their dollars – even though their immediate interests are not at stake. Citizens must view education as the most important long-term public policy area in America. To ensure that this occurs, they must be brought into the process of educational policy-making, not steered away from it. All citizens must be proud of their schools, and that pride must be developed, nurtured and sustained.

Citizens who see their school as the center of their community are apt to treat it more kindly. The center point of public life in America is democracy. The center point of democracy in Vermont is town meeting. It is time to rejoin the citizens and their schools – to bring education back into the democratic process. The future of both depends on it.

and sick. In recent decades, however, towns have lost much decision-making power to the state and federal governments.

In some cases, this transfer of local discretion to a larger entity has been appropriate. Water and air, for example, do not respect town or state lines; environmental issues must be considered from a broader perspective. But even in this area we may have been hasty in handing over all of the decision-making power. For example, having instituted consistent standards on large industrial and municipal pollution sources, environmentalists are now returning to the idea that water quality needs to be managed on a local watershed basis. Air pollution is a similar case: After standards are set to handle large pollution sources and vehicles, reducing risks from toxic air pollutants will be addressed best on a locality-by-locality basis.

Many other nagging public policy issues, from health care to public safety to transportation to the treatment of criminals (e.g. community diversion), will benefit from active local participation. The only way these issues can be managed at the local level is to maintain and build the capacity of local citizens to participate. The collective needs of society are expanding. There is plenty that we can do, and should do, at the local level if we choose the issues carefully and wisely. How best to consider these choices?

First, we must remember that history does not evolve in straight lines. There is no unseen force mandating a continuation of centralized authority. Human beings make history. We make history. Vermont has one of the most democratic and accessible state legislatures in America – the legislature is us! – and if we want to reassert our control over appropriate matters, all we need is the collective will to do so.

The term "local control" no longer carries the divisive meaning it once did. Many citizens of different political parties, from right to left to somewhere in the middle, now view local control as a positive expression of democratic hope and political efficiency.

In short, the political raw material necessary to return much of the work of democracy to the community level is within our grasp.

The authority of our communities was not always taken away. Many times we gave it away. We gave it away because we felt that the decline of localism and the rise of centralism (and the loss of democracy that went with it) was inevitable and we were helpless to stop it. It is not, and we can.

Throughout America and around the world, a new truth is emerging. Although it is almost impossible to detect it within the images cast by multi-national corporations and the nations that host them, at the grass roots where the people live, big is being replaced by small. We stand just past the summit of the age of giantism – more reason why many view the future from a centralist perspective. But the world is moving away from this summit. It is behind us as we descend into the green valleys of home and the humanity of localism, diversity and democracy that awaits us there. History is on our side now. It is time to join its hopeful journey. For in this journey lies the future of town meeting.

Chapter 9

TOWN MEETING FACT OR FICTION?

*The principal advantage of a democracy is a general
elevation in the character of the people.*

◆ James Fenimore Cooper

Town meeting is very different from other public gatherings, and it shows. You might be surprised by what studies say about the way we "do democracy" in our towns.

(1) True or false? Small-town people don't speak out much at town meeting.

False. We all know that speaking in public makes most of us a bit nervous. But this nervousness is apt to be found across any population, rural or otherwise. Towns brimming with rural folks – even those taciturn native Vermonters of popular lore – are as likely to have lively discussions at town meeting as any other Vermont town. Sometimes more likely! You might think it's too dangerous in a small town to ruffle feathers by speaking out at town meeting. Not so. Perhaps it's because town meeting has taught Vermonters that we need to speak out to make a difference. Or perhaps we've learned, deep down, that while individual differences may come and go, a community lasts.

(2) True or false? Only the privileged classes have time for town meeting.

False. There is no link between a town's attendance at or verbal participation in its town meeting and any of its economic indicators (like people's occupation, income or number of college degrees). Interestingly, studies do show a strong link between these indicators and participation in other forms of democracy. (For example, higher-income citizens are much more likely to go to a voting booth and vote.) But these findings just don't hold up for town meeting. Whether our communities are white collar, blue collar or wool plaid collar, we're just as likely to show up and speak out on Town Meeting Day. Vermonters should be proud of this. Class bias of any kind diminishes democracy.

(3) True or false? People come to town meeting only if everyone there is "just like me."

False. There is no link between whether a town is diverse – that is, home to people from a variety of social and economic backgrounds – and whether people there attend town meeting. And actually, social and economic complexity may work in favor of a vibrant discussion. In towns with rich diversity, the people who attend town meeting are somewhat more likely to speak out than those in towns where everyone has the same background.

(4) True or false? Town meeting solves all the problems of political disenfranchisement.

False. No, the sad fact is that the Vermont town has been no more successful in engaging the deeply suffering rural poor in town meeting than America's inner cities have in bringing very poor people to the voting booth. Likewise, however, it is likely that the very wealthy at the opposite end of the spectrum stay away from town meeting in equal proportions. The good news of town meeting lies in the middle. Across America, citizens with very modest education levels and below-modest incomes are voting and participating in public life less and less. But at town meeting, working-class Vermonters often participate in ways that most Americans of all classes can only dream about.

(5) True or false? The potential for conflict drives people away from town meeting.

False. In fact, the statistics show the opposite. Besides town size, the most reliable predictor of good attendance at town meeting is the presence of controversial issues on the warning. Town meeting offers Vermonters a valuable training ground to deal with their differences constructively. When there are real issues to be addressed, and we have the power at the local level to address them, Vermonters roll up their sleeves and dig in.

(6) True or false? Vermonters don't like rudeness at town meeting.

True. Enough said.

(7) True or false? Town meeting process is just too complicated for most people.

Well, now. Let's keep in mind that Vermonters of all stripes have been coming down out of the hills to conduct town meetings for well over 200 years, and most of them didn't have master's degrees. Throughout Vermont's history, most state leaders have gotten their start by participating in town affairs. Rather than being too complicated, town meeting is an education in and of itself – as Jefferson himself said, it is a critical training ground for participatory democracy.

Chapter 10

FREQUENTLY ASKED QUESTIONS ABOUT TOWN MEETING

*Some people come in from out of town and think there's
a rule for everything. Before long, though,
they find out that, no, they have to talk
with their neighbor to solve their problems.*

◆ Yvette "Effie" Brown, Craftsbury town clerk

1. Why can't we have absentee ballots for town meeting?

With ballot-box elections and other Australian ballot
votes, any voter can request an absentee ballot and vote at
a different time and place. But there is no such thing as an
absentee ballot for articles that will be discussed on the floor
at town meeting. And for good reason.

One of the great advantages of the town meeting
structure is the ability to amend from the floor. How can
we offer a pre-printed ballot on a question that has not yet
been completely formed by the town's legislators – its citizens? The legislators
simply must be present to make the decisions.

2. But what about people who just can't attend town meeting?

Without a doubt, this is the hardest question about town meeting.
Because to participate in town meeting, you have to show up.

But there are people with legitimate reasons not to attend, some of
them heart-wrenchingly so. What about military people stationed overseas,
or people who are infirm and homebound? And what about people who work
in places that just can't go unstaffed, like hospitals?

There is no single, perfect answer to this problem. But Vermonters can
make changes that will help significantly. First, everyone who wants to attend
town meeting must be able to get time off from work to do so (see "A Day
for Democracy," p. 70). And we should pursue efforts, within limits, to allow
town meeting participation from afar (see next question).

Finally, we add: Nobody said town meeting was perfect. We only said
we've never seen anything better. When a new model of self-governance
comes along that has all of the advantages of town meeting, *and* harnesses
the minds of every last voter on the checklist, we'll be first in line to try it.

3. Can technology help town meeting?

We can imagine a day when town meetings will have participation from afar. With the aid of technology, voters could hear and see the meeting, speak and even vote, all in real time. These technologies could solve the problem of some who cannot currently attend: the military person overseas or elsewhere in the United States, or the aged or ill homebound voter. Under current law, a person has to be present at town meeting to vote. But with changes in either town charters or state statute, these innovations could be incorporated.

When these proposals arrive, we will urge caution. We say, follow the model of the handicapped parking place (a few spots for those in need) rather than the model of the absentee ballot (available to all for any reason). In addition to financial considerations (How would we be sure everyone had access to the technology?), there are democratic considerations. We should enthusiastically support efforts to allow participation by those who cannot, for legitimate reasons, travel. But we should also do everything we can to maintain the face-to-face discussions and neighbor-to-neighbor problem solving that build both democratic skill and a sense of community. As anybody who has ever participated in a conference call knows: Technology works, but being there is better.

> *"People realize the beauty of voting from the floor – you can make the change right then and there. We do make amendments from the floor quite often."*
>
> Bob Greenough,
> North Hero selectman

Besides, what about the potluck dinner?

•••••

Other technological innovations are less problematic. For instance, one thing that slows down town meeting is conducting paper ballots. Paper ballots (secret ballots) are critical to the process, for they allow people to vote in private when they feel the need to. Available now are inexpensive hand-held "consensors" that could be purchased by the town. If a call came for a secret ballot, the townspeople could vote instantaneously without leaving their seats, saving 15 to 30 minutes. There are downsides: Walking up to vote can be a refreshing break and an opportunity to catch up with neighbors.

Ultimately, adopting or rejecting these innovations should be up to the towns, and town meeting participants will choose the tools best suited to strengthening their democratic process.

4. What is the best date for town meeting?

Traditionally, Town Meeting Day has been the first Tuesday in March, as per state law. In an effort to offer more flexibility, legislators changed state law to allow the meeting to be held on the three preceding days.

A few towns have experimented with a Saturday town meeting. Data are limited, but what we have seen is not promising. It turns out that as much as people don't like missing work time, people don't like missing play time either. For example, Jericho saw participation plummet during the four years (1995-98) it held town meeting on Saturday; when it returned to Tuesdays, participation went back to (and even surpassed) previous levels.

The Jericho example may also point out another trend: the relationship between schools' spring break and Town Meeting Day. Their Saturday town meeting fell during school vacation, a time when many families travel, perhaps partially accounting for the lower meeting attendance. Even towns with Tuesday town meetings may experience this draw-down, if school break week immediately precedes Town Meeting Day; after all, if Tuesday is also a school holiday, the lure of extending vacation and skipping town meeting beckons. When they time their school break, school districts need to consider its effect on democracy. Here is a good time to consider the "democratic impact statement" (discussed in Chapter 15).

While we must think carefully about the date of the meeting, it doesn't appear to be the most important factor in determining participation. Factors like Australian ballot and what's on the warning are far more important.

5. What is the best time of day for town meeting?

The answer will probably be different for every town. Data show that some towns have increased participation after switching to night meetings, but more have seen a decrease after the switch. In no case do we know for sure that either trend was linked *only* to the timing switch.

Two important facts do stand out, however. First, evening meetings tend to lower women's attendance. Bad weather also tends to lower attendance more for evening meetings than for day meetings.

Ultimately, the decision must be made by your town's voters. Whether your voters are primarily commuters, people who work locally, people who make their own schedules and other considerations will help guide you. If you do make a change, keep track of attendance to see if you've made the right decision. Again, while we must consider timing, it is not the most critical issue. Whether Australian ballot is used and the content of the warning have a much larger impact.

6. Should we move town meeting to a different time of year because of March weather?

We don't know of any evidence to suggest that moving Town Meeting Day to avoid late-season storms would improve participation. Truly lousy driving weather does reduce participation (especially at night meetings), but so does really great weather. And we have to assume that the traditional town meeting date offers the benefits of statewide pre-publicity, not to mention people's habits and traditions. In any case, the time of year is probably not the most critical factor. The content of the meeting is much more important.

7. If all the voters on our checklist don't fit into our town hall, does that mean our town is too big for town meeting?

No. And furthermore, you're not alone. From town halls to church basements, fire stations to school gyms, all Vermont town meeting spaces have one thing in common: They're too small to hold all of the registered voters.

Is this ideal? Obviously not. But here in Vermont, we are realists, and the real question is, is your town hall's size limiting the number of people who attend? Each town has to judge this individually, and if citizens feel like sardines, your town may decide to expand your community space.

But when we're compiling ways to improve attendance at town meeting, expanding the meeting hall doesn't even make the list. Data show that Vermonters attend town meeting when their presence matters – even if the meetings are more crowded.

"The year we had the worst snowstorm ever on Town Meeting Day, people couldn't get to work. So we had the most people ever at Town Meeting. And they enjoyed themselves!"

Joyce Morin,
Bakersfield town clerk

If you're concerned that you'll be so successful in improving attendance that your hall will burst, know that there is no legal reason your town meeting has to be held in your town. For instance, the regional high school in the next town is a legitimate option and will work until you build that town hall addition.

8. How do I bring up an issue at town meeting that is important to me but that isn't germane to anything that's on the warning?

Paul Gillies, who fielded questions from Vermonters about town meeting for 12 years as the deputy secretary of state, tells us that this is one of the most persistent town meeting questions. Answer: You can't.

The reason is clear. Our town meeting process is designed so that we'll arrive knowing what we're going to address and be prepared to address it. Amendments are fine; ambushes aren't. If there is a matter you just want to get off your chest, bring it up under the "new business" article. But remember that even this article cannot be used for taking binding town action. If you have something you want town meeting to take up for official and binding action, petition to get it on the warning ahead of time.

But what about the folks who attend town meeting, suddenly wake up to what they perceive as the real problems of the town and want to address them? This civic enthusiasm should be put to work! Use the energy inspired by town meeting to stay engaged throughout the year. You can work to get your idea implemented through related town structures, call a special town meeting or get it on the warning for next year.

9. Every year it seems like someone wants to pass an article about stopping war or impeaching the president. Should we discuss things at town meeting that towns really have no control over?

Town meeting is a legislative body, but like any legislative body its authority has limits. The Vermont Legislature can pass a Vermont state budget, but it can't tell Wyoming or Russia what to do. Likewise, a town meeting can pass a town budget, but its opinion on nuclear disarmament has no authority.

Yet many of the "advisory articles" placed on town meeting warnings have, arguably, had some effect. Many advocacy groups have employed town meeting votes to "send a message" to Montpelier or Washington, D.C.

Voting on advisory items may actually raise interest in town meeting, and that's fine. If an article is important enough, it will be addressed. If not, someone will move to table the motion, there will be a relieved vote to do so, and the meeting will move on.

The state and the nation have confidence in advice from town meetings because of our success in self-government. Our occasional town meeting advisory votes will have relevance only as long as our town meeting governing – on issues we *do* have the power to resolve – remains vibrant.

Part II

TAKING ACTION:
Your Town,
Your Meeting

*"Of the many things we have done
to democracy in the past,
the worst has been the indignity
of taking it for granted."*
◆ Max Lerner

Chapter 11

TEN THINGS YOU CAN DO NOW TO IMPROVE YOUR TOWN MEETING

*The principles upon which democracy rests
are as everlasting as the hills, but they must
be applied to new conditions as they arise.*

◆ William Jennings Bryan

You can take action in your town today to make your town meeting better attended and town meeting discussion even more vibrant. Here are ideas from across the state that any citizen can initiate.

1. Highlight the issues

Hot issues are one of the most important factors in determining whether people come to town meeting. You knew this already: Vermonters turn out when they know something interesting and important is going to happen.

In the interest of democracy, we're tempted to suggest that every town invent a provocative warning item (Ban alcohol within town limits? Choose your explosive issue!) just to get folks off their couches. But you don't need to be this devious. Almost every town meeting has *something* interesting happening; it's just that too often the most tantalizing discussion starters are tucked away within the bowels of the budget and are never even noticed.

How to do it: Selectboard members can choose key budget items and make them separate articles, to make sure every citizen knows they are on the warning. Enterprising town leaders interested in improving participation have tried this, and it works. And if selectboard members are unwilling to attract attention to pet items, citizens need to make this request loud and clear.

School boards may want to do this as well, but are precluded by law from doing so. This needs to be changed. In the meantime, school boards can at least sponsor a "sense of the community" resolution to guide them in their final budget preparations. While lacking the force of law, it would be good for democracy and sound public policy. No school board wants to force policies on an unwilling public. Better to find common ground through a town meeting debate whereby changes could be made to resolve legitimate complaints.

Most importantly, when local leaders and community groups have a choice of whether to decide in a small group or bring it up at town meeting, do your town a favor: Take it to the people.

2. Arrange for child care during town meeting

Happily, one of the most important methods proven to increase town meeting attendance is also relatively simple: Provide child care during the meeting. Statistics show that this can improve attendance measurably, especially among women. While children's attendance at town meeting should be encouraged, most small children won't have the patience for the full meeting, and offering child care will help parents participate more fully.

How to do it: In many communities, child care is organized not by town officials, but by a local group, which in turn can reap the benefit of collecting donations from grateful parents. Organizing groups include Girl/Boy Scouts, church youth clubs and the PTA. Some high schools have a community service requirement encouraging students to help out in such activities. Whoever organizes the child care should keep the following points in mind:

- Be certain a responsible adult supervisor is present at all times.
- Be sure the space chosen is a safe one, with toys and preferably organized activities. Children's videos can be an easy addition.
- Ideally, have child care in a location that is easily accessible so parents can check on kids during the meeting.
- Be sure the town or host group's insurance covers child care.
- Publicize the availability of child care ahead of time where parents will see it. Parent-friendly locations include preschool playgroups, school and church bulletin boards, the school newsletter that goes home to parents and in a prominent place in the town report.

3. Skip the microphones if possible

Yes, microphones at town meeting can increase our ability to hear each other, and that's good. However, they can also increase people's already-high anxiety about speaking in public. Our advice: Skip the mikes if you can.

How to do it: When recognized by the moderator, people should be reminded to stand up and speak clearly from wherever they are in the room.

Or, next-best option: If your meeting hall or gym has terrible acoustics and really needs microphones, we suggest these ideas used by many towns across Vermont:

- Don't use a stationary mike that people have to walk to the front of the room to use. This increases people's anxiety and decreases participation. Waiting in line to speak is bad enough; worse is the microphone that people walk to *after* they are recognized, adding long pauses to the meeting.

WELCOME, NEW VOTERS!

Our communities are the keepers of democracy. It is here at the town level that we administer citizenship – here that our names are added to the carefully maintained voter checklists and here that we vote, whether for town constable or U.S. president. Becoming a voter is a rite of passage that happens in our towns and can be celebrated by our towns.

A committee of citizens (perhaps working with a high school teacher) could encourage new voters to attend their town meeting the year they reach voting age. Here, they can be asked to rise and be recognized. There would be a round of applause — or even a certificate of welcome from the town. After all, when we register to vote, we aren't just filling out a form; we are becoming citizens. And what better and more memorable place to do it than at town meeting?

- Use a cordless mike (or better yet two – one on each side of the room). Appoint "runners" who trot the mike around as people are recognized by the moderator. Some towns use students as runners (a great way to expose youth to town meeting); other towns assign the job to noted officials to help build connection between elected officials and the town meeting process.
- Rent or buy a *good* sound system. A scratchy, squeaking mike is worse than none at all. It may cost a few bucks, but a better democracy is worth it.

4. Enjoy food together

The best-attended town meetings include food. And small wonder. Breaking bread together has a long history of bringing people closer. A town clerk of one high-attendance town recalled, "The secret is refreshments. Either the Grange or the school puts on a lunch. There are always doughnuts around the edges – I think that's the preschool. The Girl Scouts deliver the cookies that have been ordered." Recalled another clerk, "One year we didn't have food, and it was terrible! That was the only year I can say our attendance dropped off some."

How to do it: Food may be arranged either by local officials or volunteer groups. In many towns, a meal is served during or just after town meeting. In some towns, everyone brings a potluck dish to share; in others, morning coffee, afternoon snacks or a full meal is served by a local group as a fund-raiser.

Even simply placing a candy on each chair can help remind people that town meeting is a *celebration* of democracy.

Even towns that vote by Australian ballot can include food; in Shelburne, a community meal accompanies the Monday night informational meeting.

Don't be discouraged by the lack of facilities to serve a meal. In Strafford, a delicious potluck lunch is served despite the fact that their hall has no running water, and no kitchen, and the only heat source is the woodstoves!

5. Build an agenda that encourages attendance and participation throughout

If an article merits being on the warning, it merits the group's best attention. Town leaders should construct the meeting agenda with an eye toward full public participation.

How to do it: The agenda will create the rhythm for town meeting, so pace your articles accordingly. Which items can be worked through quickly at the beginning, to give participants a sense of momentum? Which are likely to generate lively discussion? Remember that we all lose brainpower – and town meetings often *lose participants* – right after a meal. If you put the hottest item just before a break, your post-break attendance is likely to plummet.

For the record, the best-attended town meetings in Vermont have school meetings embedded in the town meeting. Often the school items are simply included in the town meeting warning. Other towns do it this way: Town meeting begins in the morning (usually 9 a.m. or 10 a.m.) and work begins on the warning. After some time has passed (usually about an hour) the moderator adjourns the town meeting and opens the school meeting. When school business is finished, the town meeting is reconvened and proceeds until its business is finished.

Here is a "no-no." Some towns schedule their town meetings to begin in the morning and their school meetings to begin after lunch or vice versa. Three things may happen – all of them bad. (1) Town meeting is hurried to finish by noon. (2) People interested only in "town" business leave at lunch and do not return for the afternoon meeting. (3) People interested only in "school" business don't show up until after lunch, usually missing the town meeting altogether.

Regardless of your town's timing, we can all learn from this pattern: Attendance is often more stable throughout the meeting if you ensure that multiple, diverse interests are addressed throughout the agenda; enjoy some food together; and save an interesting article or two for the end.

6. Help make an excellent town report

The annual town report must, by statute, include certain official information. In addition, however, the report serves as the handbook for, and even the invitation to, town meeting. Local officials and citizen volunteers can work together to make sure the town report fills all of these roles effectively.

How to do it: Town leaders are ultimately responsible for the official contents of this report. However, community members can offer much-needed time and expertise to make the town report an appealing invitation to local democracy.

Many improvements can be achieved with little or no additional expense – just some volunteer enthusiasm. In Hartland, the Conservation Commission hosts an annual photo contest with a different theme every year, and the winning shot graces the cover of the town report. Other towns have used historical photos and maps to encourage citizens to peruse the pages.

Data can be more easily understood through good charts and graphs, and creating them is a specific task that a community volunteer could take on, if needed. Some towns solicit illustrations from local artists. Others have expanded the usual list of town officials to include phone numbers, e-mail addresses and additional key community contacts.

"The auditors have tried to make our town reports fun. They'll have pictures from different parts of the town, or historic photos. People look at the pictures, and then they might read the report!"

Cora Baker, Highgate town clerk

Excellent guidelines have been developed to inspire towns to produce thoughtful and creative town reports. There is even a town report contest to honor the most innovative. For information, contact the Vermont Institute for Government.

7. Publicize, publicize, publicize

With so much competition for our attention, it's not surprising that some Vermonters fail to realize that Town Meeting Day has rolled around again. If local democracy is to have a chance against the multi-media advertising of competing events, we'll need to go beyond the legally required postings.

How to do it: The more appealing the town report's cover "invitation" to town meeting, the better. If the town report isn't mailed to everyone, newspaper postings will meet legal requirements – but they are a poor substitute for a direct invitation to a gathering. Towns that want better engagement from their citizens may want to consider more creative publicity.

Some towns that do not want to go to the expense of sending the full town report to everyone use innovative techniques to get voters' attention. Middlebury distributes a newsprint summary of the budget, with a notice that a complete town report may be requested. Several other towns send postcard notices with the tax bill noting that the town report is available. Towns that choose not to send the town report to all taxpayers should make an extra effort to highlight the town meeting, however, and make sure that all voters are well aware of the warning items.

(For more ideas, see the box on "Creative Publicity" on page 60.)

CREATIVE PUBLICITY

Publicizing town meeting doesn't have to be expensive. And it's an excellent opportunity for volunteers to collaborate with town officials.

In Huntington, which has one of Vermont's best-attended town meetings for its size, Town Clerk Juli Lax is diligent about alerting citizens about everything from how to put items on the warning to specifics about the meeting itself. She maintains a **town Web site** that received 1,900 hits in less than a year. And, she laughs, "I put **posters** up everywhere! The town office, the two stores, the school, the post office – before town meeting, the post office guy gets so mad at me!"

Towns that have a regular **newspaper or newsletter** that carries local news are lucky; here, town officials or volunteers can remind people about the meeting, as well as offer background or even a variety of viewpoints on warning items. Develop a relationship with your newspaper, and learn how editors would like to receive information from you (whether through press releases, suggesting contacts for them or other means). Likewise, if there is a **radio** or **cable television channel** that features local news, call to see how to get your material on the air. Many towns have regular **school newsletters** that go home to parents, **church newsletters** and so on; reminders about deadlines and meetings can be featured here for free.

What are the **gathering places** in your town? The post office? The store? The school? Be sure to post information where people actually gather, even if the gatherings are informal. For example, rural Newark is not alone in having its garbage dumpster as the true information trading post on weekend mornings. Joan Bicknell, Newark town clerk, asserts, "If anyone ever wants to have a revolution, you gotta hit all the dumpsters. People go there to talk about everything!"

Bakersfield has an erasable **white-board** by the front door of the town offices, and anyone driving by can read what's coming up next. One town clerk makes it a point to **ask every citizen** who comes into her office what he or she thinks about the town meeting warning; she notes, "I don't want to sway anyone, but I do want to know that they've read it." And never underestimate **word-of-mouth**. In one high-attendance town, the town clerk admits, "I know the busybodies in town – the controversy people – and I make sure they know what's on the warning. I know they'll make sure *everyone* else knows!"

8. Include elements of celebration

Town meeting is government. But it is also the annual gathering of community members and an excellent opportunity to celebrate your town and everything we do for each other during the year. Take a few moments before or during the meeting to acknowledge what's great about your town.

How to do it: In many towns, moderators take advantage of the phrase "Unless there is an objection …" to include a moment of non-business in the proceedings. Other towns take a moment just before town meeting officially convenes for upbeat community-related items, such as a five-minute slide show of the opening of a new park or a brief presentation from students or a town committee.

9. Say "thank you"

Appreciation is one of the most valuable incentives on Earth, and it doesn't have to cost a penny. Towns wanting to increase participation can start by publicly acknowledging those who participate now.

How to do it: In many towns, the town report is dedicated to a special person or group as a show of gratitude. Often a photo is featured, and sometimes it's kept a surprise until the last minute. A brief speech in the person's honor can be included at town meeting.

"Town meeting should be fun, and ours is."
Tim Nisbet, Greensboro moderator

In Greensboro, the much-anticipated Greensboro Award goes to an honored citizen and is presented, "if there is no objection," after the third article, before any controversial items come up. In Stowe, the Conservation Commission uses town meeting as its opportunity to make an annual Conservation Award. And in Hyde Park, the moderator makes a point of saying a simple thank you to the businesses that allow their employees to take time off to attend town meeting.

10. Remember that it takes a team to make a great town meeting

A successful town meeting is never just one person's creation. Leaders and citizens must share responsibility in order to have shared success.

How to do it: Support each other. For example, in some towns the selectboard has the moderator check over the warning before it goes out, to ensure that articles are clearly written. During the meeting, the moderator should be able to depend on the clerk and other officials who know the process well to point out errors and correct them quickly. Often, selectboard and school board members will split among themselves the tasks of making presentations and answering questions.

In addition, town officers should actively seek out community volunteers. Citizens can assist with everything from helping to shape the content of the meeting and contributing to the town report to coordinating food and child care. In many towns, community groups have taken on such tasks completely over the years, freeing up officials for other duties.

More great ideas (Why stop at 10?):

11. Encourage new participation

In East Montpelier, volunteers scour the checklist for new voters. A few weeks before Town Meeting Day, new voters receive a postcard not only giving them the heads-up about their first town meeting, but inviting them to come to the meeting a half-hour early to share coffee and to get acquainted.

Some of the new names on the checklist will be people who have just moved to town, and it's always nice to welcome them. But the welcome can be an even more critical element for young, first-time voters. Communities can make a special effort to identify these new voters, warmly inviting their participation and perhaps offering a brief introductory program with their age group in mind. After all, 80 percent of 80-year olds vote, but only 20 percent of 20-year olds vote. At the community level, we can work to change this troubling trend, person by person.

12. Explain the rules

Some of the jargon of Robert's Rules of Order can be intimidating to the first-time town meeting participant. Good moderators try to make sure that old-timers and newcomers alike understand the process as it moves along, but offering an overview of the basics can be an additional help. In some towns, an overview of Robert's Rules is included in the town report or in the pre-town meeting edition of the local newsletter; in others, a flier goes on every chair explaining some of the key points. In any case, you can remind citizens of the most important "rule" in big bold letters: "If you have a question, just raise your hand and ask." (For samples of Robert's Rules overviews used by towns, contact the Vermont Institute for Government.)

13. Host living room meetings

In one Vermont town, citizens who were concerned that attendance at town meeting was lagging hosted a series of "living room meetings" several weeks before Town Meeting Day. These weren't formal pre-town meetings but neighborly get-togethers over coffee. The invitation list was made up of neighbors of all political persuasions who no longer attended (or had never attended) town meeting. The agenda: to discuss what town meeting is and why it's different from a public hearing; to go over points of particular interest on this year's warning; and to emphasize that every single citizen in town is invited and can make a difference. The meetings not only helped connect neighbors, but also brought a number of new faces to town meeting.

14. Make the room welcoming

While our municipal buildings are workplaces, they also represent our community. The more welcoming we make democracy, the more people will

THE GREENSBORO AWARD

In Greensboro, the person who will receive the annual Greensboro Award is a closely guarded secret. Selectboard members take nominations for the award each year, but the recipient they select (or recipients – sometimes they just can't narrow it down to one person) is not revealed until Town Meeting Day.

The awards have been given for some 20 years, and the recipients "can be anyone," explains Town Clerk Bridget Collier. "Sometimes it's a lifetime achievement award – sometimes it's just someone who everybody likes!" Originally the recipient received a plaque; nowadays, recipients receive a glass vase made by a local artisan. A plaque in town hall lists all the winners over the years.

"Too often, you find out about people's accomplishments in their obituaries," says moderator Tim Nisbet. "It's kind of nice to know about them when they're alive!"

No wonder Greensboro has one of the best-attended town meetings per capita. Who would want to miss the look of surprise on the recipient's face?

participate. Consider putting a vase of flowers in front of the moderator's podium or hanging artwork on the walls. How about starting a guest sign-in book, which would be fun to look at as the years go by? In Middlesex, a volunteer group cleans Town Hall before town meeting to make sure it is at its best. In Greensboro, instead of arranging the chairs in rows, meeting organizers arrange the chairs around tables. And in Bolton, local musicians even entertain town meeting-goers during their meal.

15. Highlight the work of the year

Town meeting is a great opportunity for various local groups to show off their year's work, even if they don't have an article on this year's warning. Many towns offer display tables around the edges of the meeting space, with room on the walls for posters. Municipal committees like the selectboard and planning commission can display maps and promote an understanding of their work. And there's no reason why non-municipal volunteer groups (historical societies, drama groups, etc.) can't show off, too – informal discussions before and after town meeting are great opportunities to build community.

16. Offer rides to town meeting

In most small towns, neighbors know each other well enough to get a ride to town meeting if they need it. As our towns grow, however, we may lose touch with each other. Gather a list of volunteers who can give rides to neighbors on Town Meeting Day, and publicize that rides are available. Even if no one takes you up on it the first year, people will appreciate knowing that you'll literally go out of your way to help them participate in local democracy.

17. Graduate voters

Here's an activity that doesn't happen on Town Meeting Day, but it can certainly have an impact on town meeting.

Graduation Day at Hazen Union High School features the usual commencement speeches and awards, but just before the diplomas are given out, there's a special feature.

"I ask students to raise their right hand and repeat with me the Voter's Oath," a ritual part of voter registration, explains social studies teacher Mike Metcalf. Metcalf makes sure all 18-year olds receive voter registration forms and even invites all parents and other audience members to register or re-register.

Metcalf, also a Greensboro Selectboard member and justice of the peace, wants more than just education; he wants engagement. Through school assignments, students are encouraged to attend town meeting. And as it launches its students into the world, Hazen Union makes sure its graduates can be heard in the democratic process.

Chapter 12

TEN THINGS YOU CAN DO OVER TIME TO IMPROVE YOUR TOWN MEETING

*Democracy is a process, not a static condition. It is becoming,
rather than being. It can easily be lost, but never is fully won.
Its essence is eternal struggle.*
◆ William H. Haste

Big changes take time. But we can start now on changes that will improve our local democracy for years to come.

1. Use the Australian ballot as little as possible

In a well-intentioned effort to include more people, many Vermont towns are destroying their town meeting institution. The question of whether to adopt the Australian ballot for town and school meetings is not as simple as "more is better."

How to do it: Ultimately, the decision is in the hands of the voters of your town – as it should be. Citizens in your town need to look at the pros and cons of the Australian ballot. Consider the discussion in Chapter 6. Whether through public discussions, media, fliers or word-of-mouth, make sure the citizens in your town have all the facts before they decide.

2. Help make Town Meeting Day a real democracy holiday

Many people are required to lose a day's pay to attend town meeting, yet attend anyway – an impressive sign of people's interest in local democracy. But it's not fair, and it has to change.

How to do it: Support and publicly recognize by name those businesses that encourage employees to participate in local democracy. Encourage lawmakers to ensure that all Vermonters who want to can receive time off from work to attend town meeting. (See "A Day for Democracy," p. 70.)

3. Combine school and town meetings

The best-attended town meetings are those that combine school and town meetings on the same day. Some towns are choosing to switch their school meeting to a separate day and/or to Australian ballot. When they do, it not only cuts into the quality of the school meeting; in addition, studies show clearly that *it will reduce attendance at the town meeting.*

How to do it: If your town is considering separating its town and school meetings, or if it already has, you will need to talk with your neighbors. Many people support separating town and school meeting because they believe it will give their town "more democracy." Have them read Chapter 6 and see if they still think so.

Take the time to develop citizen interest in bringing the school and community back together. Be sure to include those who are critical of the schools, as well as the many who no longer have kids in the school. Reach out. It will be work, but it can also be fun. And while they're not here to let you know it, great Americans from Thomas Jefferson to John Dewey to Abraham Lincoln to Franklin Roosevelt will be smiling on your efforts.

If you want your town to vote on whether to re-combine school and town meeting, ask your town clerk or selectboard member how to get an item on the warning, or contact the Vermont Institute for Government. Remember that it is remarkably easy to use the democratic process in Vermont. It is waiting for you.

4. Be an advocate for creative localism

Vermonters, both citizens and lawmakers, must recognize the connection between vibrant local democracy and community well-being. Much can be done to take advantage of and increase the power accorded to local citizens.

How to do it: Encourage state leaders to re-entrust our localities with expanded decision-making power.

In addition to urging our leaders to act, we have considerable authority to "re-localize" on our own. Many Vermont towns don't take advantage of all the powers they currently have – powers that can inspire citizen participation and enliven town meeting. Here are some examples:

- Under the law that creates conservation commissions, towns can actually be land trusts, administering gifts of land or funds for land conservation. Many towns have conservation funds set aside. Whether and how much money to allocate to these funds and how they are administered are purely local decisions.

- Many Vermont towns have funds donated by benefactors for local uses. In the early 1900s, the northern New England states made an effort to encourage the well-to-do to create such funds (most of Vermont's public libraries are a result). In the tiny town of Baltimore (pop. 250), factory worker Ella Graves left a small fund when she died in 1918 to help the needy; the fund, administered by the selectboard, now helps pay residents' medical bills! Explore your town's resources and its needs. It's never too late to consider creative uses for an existing endowment or raise money to create a new one.

TOWN MEETING AND EDUCATION

Town Meeting Day is an excellent focus for civic education, and many Vermont schools have incorporated town meeting materials into their studies. Classrooms come alive with debate over direct versus representative democracy, and some teachers are even letting students make decisions that will affect their day using a town meeting-style process.

The Vermont Secretary of State's Office offers free curriculum materials, including the "Vermont Town Meeting Coloring and Activity Book" (grades K-3), "Town Mouse and Country Mouse Go to Town Meeting" (grades 4-6) and "Town Meeting Day: A Vermont Tradition" (for middle schools), which includes curriculum materials and a teachers guide, plus supplementary materials and discussion questions.

In addition, Project Citizen-Vermont is a program designed to involve middle-school students directly in local issues, where they not only learn and practice the skills necessary to participate in a democracy but can actually affect public policy.

For information, see "Resources for Democracy & Community," p. 85.

5. Recognize the impact of population on local democracy

A town's population is proven to be *the single strongest factor* in determining attendance and participation in town meeting. The more people in your town, the smaller the percentage of registered voters who will come to, and speak at, town meeting.

How to do it: We weigh many factors when we plan for the future of our towns: environment, business, education, affordability, traffic and historic preservation being just a few. We need to add one more to the list: local democracy. When Vermont communities are considering development plans, we must keep in mind the irrefutable fact that citizen democracy works best in small towns. When the town plan comes up for revision, communities may choose to incorporate wording reflecting their value of small-town, local democracy. Or, if a town chooses to grow, citizens should take steps to offset the reduction that this growth is likely to cause in citizens' motivation to participate.

6. No matter what your town's size, cultivate small-town advantages

Small towns get better per capita participation at town meeting. But larger towns can take action to make their towns feel smaller and reap the benefit in democratic participation.

How to do it: Spread the word: Small-town connections will not just make your town friendlier; they will improve your economy, health *and* democracy. There is a lot you can do, over time, to foster small-town advantages in your community. For specific ideas, see "The Other 364 Days," p. 76.

7. Involve youth in town meeting

First impressions are lasting, and many Vermonters' memories of attending town meeting as children stay with them their whole lives. As an investment in democracy's future, you can't do better than giving kids a firsthand taste at town meeting.

How to do it: Many towns involve children in direct ways, such as arranging for a student presentation on school programs. Students can lead the civil invocation, assist with food or carry microphones to people as they are recognized to speak. Youth can also be involved indirectly, for example by featuring student artwork (perhaps with a community theme) on the walls. Students may observe a portion of town meeting with their school class or home-school group. Many educators find that town meeting can be an excellent curriculum focus.

> *"I encourage people to bring kids to town meeting. So for most kids, it's not a mystery. It's natural."*
>
> Bridget Collier
> Greensboro town clerk

8. Create a "Democracy Matters" committee in your town

We have societies to preserve our local history, commissions for conservation, bureaus for better business. Why not a committee to safeguard local democracy? These volunteer committees would keep an eye on town meeting attendance and participation, and work to improve both. While they could not be entirely responsible for protecting democracy – that's everyone's job – they could sound the alarm when it is in decline and take local action. Some of the steps outlined in this book would be a great start, but local citizens will undoubtedly come up with more and better ideas!

How to do it: Your town officials (especially the selectboard and town clerk) should be involved with this committee – many of the recommendations will affect them, and they are important to the committee's success. However, ideally it will not be led by current town officials, but by other citizens committed to democratic participation. This committee should not take stands on local issues, unless they relate directly to the democratic process. Since it's almost impossible to have a committee of non-political citizens, be sure there are participants from across the political spectrum.

The committee could work outside of government in a watchdog capacity. Alternately, the committee could be institutionalized and elected at town meeting. To do the latter, discuss the idea with people in your town, and ask the selectboard to put the proposal on the warning. Or, collect the requisite petition signatures to have the proposal put on the warning. And while you are getting the signatures, you can recruit volunteers to stand for membership on the committee.

Either way, the committee could offer a yearly public report in the town report (and perhaps briefly presented at town meeting each year) outlining attendance trends, numbers of candidates volunteering to run for office, the presence of women in town officer posts, as well as efforts to provide child care, foster cross-community communication, encourage young voters to attend and participate, and other endeavors. (For more information on creating a "Democracy Matters" committee, contact the Vermont Institute for Government.)

9. Be prepared

Leaders, be prepared: Towns with consistently successful and well-attended town meetings have this in common: Elected and appointed officials plan ahead and arrive well prepared with the information they'll need to respond to citizens' queries. For example, having the selectboard offer a brief (less than five-minute) overview of budgetary changes and what they will mean to the tax bill can be an efficient way to begin the budget discussion.

But not too prepared: When leaders offer an elaborate Power Point presentation on the budget or darken the room for a slide show on the proposed truck purchase, it can give citizens the uncomfortable impression that a decision has already been made and set in stone. Citizens should simply get the information they need to make a decision – then let the discussion begin.

Citizens, be prepared: Arrive with your town report and thoughtful questions ready. If you aren't sure how to interpret the town report, it's never cheating to call the town clerk's office in advance of the meeting and ask. (Or see the Vermont Institute for Government's helpful flier, *"How and Why to Read Your Town Report."*)

But not too prepared: You've come to town meeting to discuss the issues, hear the different points of view and then make a decision. Don't make the classic mistake of being so focused on what you are going to say that you don't listen to what others offer.

10. Resist the temptation to delegate

In the interest of efficiency, some towns appoint committees to do work that has in the past been done by town meeting participants. For example, in some towns, a funding committee reviews the requests from nonprofit groups and then submits a budget recommendation to the voters. But Vermonters don't attend town meetings just to be rubber stamps. A more lively discussion and meaningful participation at town meeting will result if the same effort is spent making sure all of the relevant information goes into the town report so voters can make an informed decision themselves.

A Day for Democracy

Back when most Vermonters were farmers, taking a break in early March for democracy fit naturally into the flow of the year. And we didn't need anyone's permission to do so.

Today, many Vermonters feel stretched between working, commuting and parenting. Between outsourcing and downsizing, some businesses have everything they can do to stay afloat. Who has the luxury of a day off for town meeting?

Our advice: Take a deep breath and slow down. Remember: We're talking about our *democracy*. Short of, perhaps, our family's health, what is more important than our freedom to rule ourselves?

Yes, democracy comes at a cost. If employees get paid time off to attend town meeting, it will cost employers. If the time off is unpaid, it will cost employees. Nothing worthwhile is free.

> *"Why do we have a Bennington Battle Day holiday, and not Town Meeting Day? It's so dumb. It ought to be a paid holiday."*
>
> Joan Bicknell, Newark town clerk

Democracy is the same as a business in one way, at least: You get what you pay for. And if we are serious about self-governance, we need to remember that the currency we pay with is time – our time. We put in our time regularly via town meeting – reviewing the books, enhancing our understanding, making changes as needed. How can we make sure that everyone who wants to can put time into this process?

What follows is a range of different ways we might ensure that anyone who wants to attend town meeting can do so. We're all for public debate on which method is best. The important thing is to do it.

Democracy Day

In our ideal world, Vermont will declare a paid holiday when offices, banks and businesses would close in a grand celebration of community life. Let's ordain it in the state constitution: "Democracy Day."* We will hold town meetings, including festive potluck meals. Larger municipalities and cities that don't have town meeting will also celebrate democracy on this day, with public forums and debates. But that's not all. There will be youth involvement, educational events, parades, concerts, and sporting events on Democracy Day (and the days leading up to it), all in celebration of Vermont's tradition of local democracy.

---

* Note: The vision of a Vermont "Democracy Day" is further detailed in "The Vermont Papers" by Frank Bryan and John McClaughry, Chelsea Green, 1989.

SOME THINGS ARE MORE IMPORTANT
THAN WORK

"**M**y father was a double amputee due to injuries sustained during the D-Day invasion of WWII. He spent two years recovering in Walter Reed Hospital. He died when I was 11 as a result of those injuries. He was very patriotic and never complained about his sacrifice to the cause of freedom and our basic rights of free speech.

"Town meeting and voting are part of our civic responsibilities as citizens. Town Meeting and Election Day are probably two of the most important days of the year. In my opinion, they're much more important than Presidents Day or Bennington Battle Day.

"As an employer, I encourage our employees to get involved by voting or participating in town meeting. I have and will always work around any employees' schedule who are willing to perform their civic duties. ... I would hate to think that my father and the thousands more who paid the ultimate sacrifice did so in vain." *Phil Scott*

Phil Scott is co-owner of Dubois Construction, a state senator (R-Washington) and a Thunder Road auto racing champion.

Institutionalize the ability to vote

Shouldn't voting be protected by state law? Under this proposal, Vermont would treat voting (including participation in town meeting) as we do jury duty: It's part of public life, and you'd get time off from work, if needed, to do it.

You'd need to prove to your employer that you're registered to vote. And if they chose, employers could request proof – for example, a letter from the town clerk – that an employee really voted and/or attended town meeting.

Not all towns hold their town meetings at the same time, or even on the same day; meanwhile, cities don't have town meetings at all. These factors would allow many critical services (hospitals, fire stations, etc.) to stagger staffing and encourage democratic participation in employees' hometowns.

Town meeting holiday, town meeting culture

Town Meeting Day is already on the books as a state holiday. However, this only means that state employees and businesses that choose to follow the state calendar get time off. Businesses do a service to their communities by honoring the Town Meeting Day holiday.

Older Vermonters remember when the only thing that was happening on Town Meeting Day was: town meeting. And it still happens today, in some of our smaller towns. This could become the case again throughout Vermont.

Regardless of the laws we pass about what we "should" do on Town Meeting Day, the final key to success will be what actions we take. Do we attend, and bring a friend? Do we honor the day and those who work all year to make it worth our effort? Do we applaud businesses that contribute to the community by encouraging employees to attend town meeting? Town meeting is our state democratic treasure; let's treat it that way.

A note to business people

We're recommending that your business be open one day fewer per year and/or that you let your employees take time off to attend town meeting. Some of you already do this and are happy to. Others might think we're nuts.

Yes, more time for democracy means less time for other things, including work. But it will have a payback, too. Keep in mind:

- Town meeting is a training ground for skills that employees can transfer to the workplace: an understanding of public process; the ability to express ideas publicly and concisely; compromise; even tolerance.
- Town meeting helps keep Vermont one of the most civic, neighborly places to live in the world. Quality of life is one of the most important advantages Vermont has in drawing businesses, and town meeting is part of that quality.
- Everyone loves a business with a strong sense of civic responsibility. Town Meeting Day is the time to show it.

Chapter 13

A WORD ABOUT MODERATING

Rely on Robert's Rules for crowd control? You can't.
You have to find a way to help people express themselves.

◆ Carl Fortune, retired town moderator, Hyde Park

Your town deserves excellent moderating. Your town meeting depends on it.

Here's how you can tell if you have an effective moderator. Is your moderator:

- Objective and fair?
- Conversant in Robert's Rules of Order?
- Able to keep the meeting in perspective and show a sense of humor?
- A capable meeting "storyteller" – that is, good at crisply summarizing, "Here's what just happened, here's what we will address next, and here's how we'll do it"?

If you don't have a good moderator, you need to get one. There are two ways to do this:

1. Give your moderator an opportunity to learn more. Moderator trainings are offered annually by the Vermont League of Cities and Towns, and this group also offers an excellent moderators' handbook. Even seasoned moderators can learn something new each year from these refresher trainings and materials.
2. Elect a new moderator. Whether this is by gently suggesting to your moderator that his or her time could be better spent in a different role, or via an all-out coup, will depend on the politics of your town.

But whatever you do, don't underestimate the need for excellence in this role.

Some suggestions for moderators

Moderating involves understanding the rules and maintaining order, but good moderators do more than just wield Robert's Rules of Order. They inspire the civility that keeps people coming back to town meeting. Here are just a few examples of how they can do it; more are available from the Vermont Institute for Government.

"COMMUNITY"
by Marshall Squier

A community is a blending place where people come together,
Not just in bright sunshine, but also in foul weather.
They see and feel a common need, neighbor giving neighbor
    a helping hand,
They take a higher road than self, a common good, a community
    that will stand.

The cougar left and now is back, the moose in Tinmouth now roam,
Like them, no matter from where or when you came, the Tinmouth
    community is our home.
Left or right, new or old, working to make this a special place,
Talking our differences out, shaking hands, discussing it with grace.

We have a place to dance and play, to meet and talk it out,
Making Tinmouth Tinmouth, that's what it is all about.
A beautiful town with mountains, farms and fresh clean air,
A special community it will always be, if all of us care.

So let's give a little here and there, all for the common good,
Work and play, laugh and dance, right here in our native wood.
A community, like a relationship, needs work to keep it strong,
Join in, take part, we all are needed to sing this song.

In addition to serving as Tinmouth's unofficial town poet, Marshall Squier is town moderator. He is the chief of Tinmouth's volunteer fire department and chair of its planning commission (both of which he helped create); he is also president of the local land trust and town constable.

Whenever possible, call people by name

Craftsbury Moderator Anne Wilson says, "I recognize everyone when they stand up to speak, either by name or I ask, 'Please identify yourself.'"

Local officials can work on this. In Craftsbury, Town Clerk Yvette "Effie" Brown says, "Before town meeting, I go through the voter checklist and check the new names, because I know the moderator or a selectboard member is going to ask me."

Detailed minutes help reinforce that participation matters. Brown also notes, "I try to get people's names in the minutes – whoever brings up the main points and the main rebuttals."

In addition to increasing a sense of civic engagement in Craftsbury, recognizing speakers by name (or asking them to identify themselves) builds community. "Then during a paper ballot," Brown observes, "people will strike up a conversation with someone they didn't know."

Go over the rules

Many of the best moderators take a moment at the beginning of the meeting to go over the most important of Robert's Rules. There is no need to go into great detail, since a good moderator will remind participants as they go along. But at a minimum, it is helpful to remind participants to address all comments to the moderator and to ask questions at any time.

Dairy farmer Paul Doton has been Barnard's moderator for many years, as was his father before him. Doton begins his meeting with a brief (two-to-three minute) overview; his notes are available from the Vermont Institute for Government.

> "[At a well-moderated town meeting] there's a feeling of community spirit and respect. People may not like each other, but they respect each other."
>
> Anne Wilson,
> Craftsbury town moderator

Enlist help

The best moderators have town clerks or other sidekicks acting as an extra set of eyes and ears during the meeting. Some enlist a parliamentarian to double-check on Robert's Rules. Moderators can also learn a lot from finding "mentor" moderators who run successful town meetings in neighboring towns and discussing techniques with them.

Remind participants about community civility

Starting town meeting on the right foot can make all the difference. In Danville, the town parliamentarian begins with an invocation for civility (see frontpiece of this book). In Tinmouth, the moderator opens the meeting by reading a new poem he writes each year about the town! (See previous page.)

Chapter 14

THE OTHER 364 DAYS

Town meeting is only one day. But here at the store,
it lasts at least two weeks. The week before,
it's "What I'm going to say…" and then
the week after, it's "What I should have said!"

◆ Myrna Tallman, co-proprietor, Tallman's Store, Belvidere

Town meeting is only one day per year. But it is
the culmination of a year's worth of budgeting and
decisions. Citizens need to understand these decisions
as the year progresses. They need to know when and
how to make their views known, so proposals arrive
at town meeting formed by broad citizen
participation. And they need to be prepared to step
up and be leaders themselves when the time comes.

We need to keep the tools of our democracy
sharpened throughout the year. To build an even better Town Meeting Day, local officials and citizens alike
have to spend the other 364 days going beyond …

… beyond the 7 p.m. public hearing

You'll be working on important issues for months leading up to a town
meeting vote. How do you keep people engaged along the way? Public
hearings are very well and good. But we all know they don't work for
everyone. Here are some techniques Vermont towns have used to think
beyond the 7 p.m. public hearing:

- If the proposal you're addressing involves a specific place in the town
  (e.g. village zoning, a historic building), host an on-site field trip. Some
  folks like maps and charts, but many people will gain a much fuller
  understanding and be able to offer more in a hands-on setting.
- Set up a booth at local events – the school fair, the church flea market,
  etc. Have a bowl of apples or candy out to show that you're actively
  inviting folks over. Be available to chat with people informally,
  one-on-one, about your project. Offer informational handouts
  with contacts.
- Publicize creatively. (For ideas, see p. 60.)

- Go where people are. Find out about the informal groups in your community – snowmobile clubs, book groups, preschool play groups where parents gather – and ask for permission to join them briefly at their next get-together. If service clubs meet regularly in your community (Rotary, League of Women Voters, etc.), request space on their agenda. Bring informational handouts with contacts.
- Organize a living room meeting in each of your town's neighborhoods. Of course your friends will know about this project, but what about the folks on the other side of town you hardly ever talk to? What about their friends? People can say – and learn – a lot in a small, relaxed setting over coffee.

… beyond the national headlines

Large-town newspapers are fine for getting the big news, but most small towns need a truly local news source. From the *Middlesex Monthly* newspaper to the *Tales of Tinmouth* flier, the *Lake Champlain Islander* to the *East Montpelier Signpost*, community newspapers and newsletters are informing citizens as well as building community. Some are printed on newsprint and take advertising. Many others are very informal – run by volunteers, with copying and distribution supported by neighborly donations. Some towns even have locally owned citizen journalism Web sites that anyone can post items on, published continually. (Check out *www.ibrattleboro.com* and *www.iputney.com*: "From Porch to Portal.") Whatever format is right for your town, citizens need a place where they can air viewpoints throughout the year, and the selectboard and other relevant groups can submit a regular letter (or minutes) so townspeople have an idea of what topics are hot.

… beyond paper

Many towns now have Web sites, featuring a range of town-related information. Of course, many people don't use the Internet, so it should not be relied upon as the sole means of getting the word out. And the Internet is no substitute for face-to-face communication. But it's a helpful communication supplement, available 24/7.

A town Web site can include town officials' contact information, committee agendas and minutes. It can list important dates, such as deadlines for getting articles on the town meeting warning, as well as details on how to do so. Here, people can save paper and a trip to the town hall by downloading forms, town plans and maps. Some towns put their whole town report on the Web site. Some towns also have candidates' pages, business listings and tourism information, as well as information on volunteer groups such as historical societies, art and youth groups, and more.

"We were answering the same questions over and over again," recalls Huntington Town Clerk Juli Lax. Now, Huntington citizens can go to the Web site for the most commonly needed information, and Lax says Web site maintenance takes only about an hour per week.

… beyond town meeting

Town meeting is convened once a year – traditionally in March. But notice that when you elect your moderator, it's not just for Town Meeting Day, but "for the ensuing year." Why is that?

Because things come up. Historically, most towns held multiple town meetings during the year, to address issues as they arose. Just as legislators sometimes go into special session, the legislators of your town – all your voters – can convene a special town meeting at any point in the year.

For details on how to petition for a special town meeting, contact your town clerk or the Secretary of State's Office. The solution to people's lack of interest in democracy isn't to have less democracy – it's to foster more and better democracy!

… and on into the community itself

When we celebrate community, we strengthen democracy.

You've known it all along. Now, social scientists have the data to prove the direct cause-and-effect link: *Small-town connections and strong community spirit will not only make your town friendlier, they will improve your local economy, health and democracy.*

There is a lot you can do, over time, to improve your sense of community and, hence, local democracy. Whatever your town's size, you can foster "small-town" advantages. How?

- Emphasize your town's identity and center.
- Celebrate your town's unique culture, historic events and historic buildings.
- Highlight your town's unique natural features.
- Improve cross-community communication.
- Create gathering places.
- Help neighbors hire neighbors.
- Enhance the connections between community and school.
- Discuss your community's values and vision for its future.

Here are just a few examples of creative community-building ideas from across the state.

Celebrating local culture

The Huntington Living Arts Festival has been an annual celebration of local art and artists, music and musicians. From photographers to metal workers, weavers to stone masons, people have displayed their talents and sold their wares, neighbor to neighbor. The whole community has enjoyed the great local food and family entertainment. After running the festival for some five years, the Huntington Valley Arts group is now moving on to organize an "open studio" tour in the area. "We find it heartening that so many individual endeavors of economic independence, so much creativity, exists within our community," organizers say.

Emphasizing town identity

Every community has its treasures, but a growing number now also has treasure maps! Many schools, as well as historical and conservation groups, are sharing their towns' villages, historic and natural sites by creating "Quests" – maps and poems that lead adventurers to key locations. In total, 164 Quests in the Upper Valley (Vermont and New Hampshire) are being enjoyed by locals and visitors alike. In Norwich, Marguerite Ames' students conducted field research and oral histories to create their Quests, which were then shared with the larger community. Says Ames, "My son never passes through the village without mentioning something he learned through the Quest."

Highlighting your town's unique natural features

Seeing a bear, moose or fox in the wild is a thrill worth sharing with neighbors. In Marlboro and Dummerston, citizens are encouraged to keep track of the wild animals they see throughout the year. Then, at town meeting, the Conservation Commission provides a map and multicolored push-pins for people to record their wildlife sightings. In addition to being useful in town planning, according to Cami Elliot-Knaggs of Dummerston, "I like to think it makes people more aware of our town and what is here. It gets people thinking." And talking. She notes, "We had to move into the hallway, there was so much conversation at our table!"

> *"I know I can go into the Hero's Welcome store every Sunday morning and catch someone. You can't escape. Unless you go in disguise, maybe."*
>
> Bob Greenough
> North Hero selectman

Improving cross-community communication

In Middlesex, the school is on one side of town, the town hall is on the other, with the interstate in between. There is no post office or town green. And many commuters spend more time in nearby Montpelier and Waterbury than they do in their hometown. In short, folks need to do a little extra to stay connected. Fortunately, the town is rich in energy, talent and good will. In 2003, volunteers published the "Middlesex Operator's Manual," 40-plus illustrated pages on how to get involved in town government, community groups and more. A volunteer-run Web site (*www.middlesex-vt.org*) features the manual and updated contacts. According to the Vermont League of Cities and Towns, "the manual is becoming a model for other towns' efforts to promote greater citizen participation."

Creating gathering places

In rural Tinmouth, "We wanted to create a gathering place and a reason to come together," explains local volunteer Cathy Reynolds. After working hard over several years to renovate a local building, volunteers organized a spring and fall concert series. "I kept saying, if you build it, they will come," says Reynolds. "Turns out I was right." Money collected at the door pays the performers, with 10 percent going to building upkeep. Reynolds reports, "Great vibes, great feedback, real music in a non-smoky atmosphere, supporting struggling, mostly-Vermont musicians … and it's fun!" The concert series is in its fifth year and going strong.

Discussing your community's values and vision for its future

Many Vermont towns have benefited from gathering citizens to explore their common values and ideas for the future. Not "town planning" per se, these gatherings can focus on everyone's interests, whether they are economic, social, environmental or some combination. Out of these visioning sessions come specific action plans and real community-building success. For a list of organizations that can help with this work in Vermont, contact the Vermont Institute for Government.

Helping neighbors hire neighbors

Tiny Middletown Springs isn't a quick drive from anyplace. So it makes a big difference if you can find someone close by who can fill a need. Every year, volunteers organize the Middletown Springs Phone and Business Directory. Everyone in town offering a service or producing goods is encouraged to have a free listing, while paid business card ads cover printing costs. Want to hire a carpenter or buy a cord of wood? Need to get a logo designed or hire a pet sitter? You can check the directory and hire your neighbor. "We first published the directory to encourage the local economy and foster a stronger sense of community," says volunteer Kimberly Mathewson. "Now, people wonder out loud, 'How did we get along without it?' I never knew there were so many talented people right here in town."

Enhancing the connections between community and school

In Bradford, students have joined with local businesses and the Conservation Commission to create an interpretive map of the community forest. Students and community members will harvest trees to build a teaching gazebo on site, and kindergartners have produced a forest ABC book to share with local day care centers. The forest is becoming an inviting resource for the whole community. Bradford is one of an increasing number of towns enjoying the advantages of "place-based education." Schoolchildren do much of their learning directly in the community, focusing on local issues and opportunities. Citizens and businesspeople become invested in students' learning. And the students are seen as the community assets they are, not only "practicing" civic skills but actually helping address local issues.

Chapter 15

A DEMOCRATIC
IMPACT STATEMENT

The besetting sin of democrats has been complacency.
◆ John Strachey

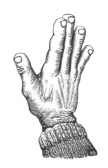

Over the years it has become more or less standard procedure: Those who propose big development projects must complete an "environmental impact statement" showing the effect their project will have on the environment – water, air, wildlife and so on. We also require similar information to assess disturbances to historical sites and buildings, increases in traffic congestion and suburban sprawl, and interruptions of scenic views.

Well and good. But what about our democracy, the process through which we govern ourselves? It does not demean our concern for our physical environment to suggest that our democratic environment deserves equal attention.

We ask those who would alter our physical environment to tell us what impact their plans would have on our capacity to hunt deer in the fall, view a 19th-century barn from a roadside, or hear the red-wing blackbird's song from the wetland across the way.

It is time that we ask private developers, as well as government officials, to make a similar assessment of their proposals' impacts on our capacity to practice democracy. This information should weigh heavily in our final decision.

Here are some cases when a "democratic impact statement" might be needed, each accompanied by a discussion-starting example of one reason why. Some of these cases are hypothetical. Others reflect policies that have already been implemented or suggested. All are listed here to provoke discussion: What impacts, positive and negative (and usually unintentional), can our actions have on local democracy?

- A developer wants to build an assisted-care facility for the aged in your town. *The town may want to plan ways for the residents to participate in town meeting.*

- The state passes a law that requires towns to have their selectboards appoint their road commissioners unless the town chooses to exercise its power to elect the commissioner at town meetings. *Such elections are often hotly contested and draw voters to town meeting.*

- The Fish and Game Department allows sale of hunting licenses at the local hardware store (and other venues) instead of the town clerk's office. *Going to a town office to purchase a license strengthens the town-citizen bond.*

- The state allows Vermont towns to piggyback a local income tax on its residents' state income tax forms to shift some of the local tax burden away from the property tax. *Such an innovation would dramatically expand citizen interest in town government.*

- An out-of-state developer proposes a large retail development outside of the traditional center of town. *This could erode sense of community and thereby weaken town meeting.*

- The state mandates the creation of a preschool program in every town. *Mandates, no matter how well meaning, can detract from democracy.*

- A proposal for the village includes a new bandstand and signs telling travelers that they have entered your village. *Such a proposal could strengthen community and thus town meeting.*

- Congress votes to discontinue federal revenue sharing to the states. *These "no-strings-attached" revenues expanded participation.*

- The selectboard of your town proposes to resume sending a town report to each citizen. *By providing more public information this would strengthen town meeting.*

- The state approves "school choice," allowing a community's children to attend different schools outside of town. *Removing families' link with their community school seriously weakens their connection to the town, and to local democratic participation.*

How a democratic impact statement would look in final form remains to be seen. Below are some examples of questions that could help us determine whether a proposal will improve or detract from democratic participation.

1. Does the proposal maintain or improve citizens' decision-making power at the community level?

Citizens are more likely to participate democratically when they are making decisions, not simply offering opinions to decision makers.

2. Does the proposal support or improve communication among different community sectors (e.g. parents with non-parents, old-timers with newcomers, etc.)?

Our democracy works better when all voices are heard, and heard by all.

3. Does the proposal help emphasize the community's history and identity?

Emphasizing what is unique about a town can help increase civic engagement.

4. Does the project highlight citizens' connection to your community center, significant landmarks and places?

Studies clearly show that suburbanization and sprawling development detract from our community connectedness and have a measurably negative effect on civic participation.

5. Will the project reduce traffic or commuting time in your town?

Studies show that every 10 minutes added to a person's daily commute reduces the time they'll be involved in community affairs by 10 percent.

6. Does your project offer people an entertainment alternative to television?

Nothing – not low education, not poverty, not long commutes – is worse for civic engagement and social connection than dependence on television for entertainment. Every additional hour of television viewing per day means about a 10 percent reduction in civic engagement. And you thought the town band, community potluck or pick-up soccer game was just a fun idea?

These and other questions must be asked, if our democracy is to be preserved. At this point, a Vermont democratic impact statement is only a suggestion for the future. But the ideas behind it are alive right now, for every citizen who values democracy. Start today to ask these and other relevant questions. Ask them of yourself as you read the newspaper; ask your neighbors as you chat over the back fence; ask leaders as you explore proposals at public meetings. And be sure the answers are included in every decision your community makes.

Chapter 16

ONWARD

*If the spirit of liberty should vanish in other parts of the Union,
and support of our institutions should languish,
it could all be replenished from the generous store
held by the people of this brave little state of Vermont.*
◆ Calvin Coolidge, 1928

Democracy. As a global enterprise, its principles rival those of the world's great religions. Within the extremes of sanctimony and sincerity, good and evil, and war and peace that this beautiful word has inspired, there resides an incandescent truth.

Democracy is the world's best hope for survival. The fundamental notion that ordinary citizens can come together, find common ground and act in their collective best interests – in a word, can *govern* themselves – must be so, if the dearest dreams of the human race are ever to be fulfilled.

Town meeting *is* democracy – arguably, the world's most perfect working example. And one thing is for certain: Nowhere is town meeting practiced more thoroughly and completely as it is here.

This generation of Vermonters will choose whether to keep or to lose town meeting. Will the democratic inheritance of our brave little state be passed on to the next generation intact?

The decision is in our hands.

Appendices

APPENDIX 1: RESOURCES FOR DEMOCRACY AND COMMUNITY

Center for Rural Studies
A nonprofit, fee-for-service research organization that addresses social, economic and resource-based problems of rural people and communities. They serve as the U.S. Census Bureau's Vermont State Data Center, and make a broad range of town-level data available free on their Web site. Address: 207 Morrill Hall, University of Vermont, Burlington, VT 05405. Web site: http://crs.uvm.edu/

League of Women Voters of Vermont
A nonpartisan group promoting political responsibility through informed and active participation in government. Activities include sponsoring candidates' debates, producing the "Vermont Citizens Guide to State Government," and lobbying on democracy-related issues. Tel: 802-657-0242. Web site: www.lwvofvt.org.

Project Citizen-Vermont
A middle school civic education program designed to develop interest in public policy-making. Students select a community or state need, then pursue an investigation leading to solutions and an action plan. The Center for Civic Education is the national sponsor (www.civiced.org), and in Vermont, the Vermont League of Cities and Towns is a co-sponsor. For information about the program, professional development opportunities, and activities, contact: William H. Haines, State Coordinator, 339 Elmore Road, Worcester, VT 05682. Tel: 802-229-9303. www.projectcitizenvt.org

Vermont Institute for Government
A nonprofit organization dedicated to improving educational opportunities for local officials and the public. Offers free informational pamphlets on a variety of town-meeting-related topics. Address: 617 Comstock Road, Suite 5, Berlin, VT 05602-9194. Tel: 802-223-2389. Web site: www.vtinstituteforgovt.org

Vermont League of Cities and Towns
VLCT is a nonprofit, nonpartisan organization owned by Vermont's municipal governments. All 246 Vermont towns are members, and VLCT services are offered to municipal officials. Address: 89 Main St., Suite 4, Montpelier, VT 05602-2498. Tel: 802-229-9111 or 800-649-7915. Web site: www.vlct.org.

Vermont Secretary of State's Office
This office offers a wealth of information regarding issues related to democracy. Extensive Web site offers many relevant links, materials for incorporating town meeting into school curricula, and more. Address: 26 Terrace Street, Montpelier, VT 05609-1101. Tel: 802-828-2363. Web site: www.sec.state.vt.us.

Vital Communities
Vital Communities has a number of programs that can serve as models for Vermont towns seeking to strengthen their sense of community. Among them are their "Valley Quest" and "Village Quest" community treasure hunt programs. Publications for community and school groups are available. Address: 104 Railroad Row, White River Jct. VT 05001. Tel: 802-291-9100. Web site: www.vitalcommunities.org.

Additional Web sites:
For more information on proportional and semi-proportional voting methods, go to www.fairvote.org.

APPENDIX 2: FOR FURTHER READING

- **Barber, Benjamin R.** *Strong Democracy.* Berkeley: University of California Press, 1984.
  An important and creative analysis of the decline of citizenship in America and what can be done about it.
- **Bellah, Robert N., William M. Sullivan, Ann Swindler, and Steven Tipton.** *Habits of the Heart.* New York: Harper & Rowe, 1985.
  One of the most influential books on the roots of the American democratic impulse published in the post-World War II period.
- **Bookchin, Murray.** *The Rise of Urbanization and the Decline of Citizenship.* San Francisco: Sierra Club Books, 1987.
  A sweeping and eloquent historical analysis of the relationship between democracy and the mega-city.
- **Bryan, Frank M.** *Real Democracy: The New England Town Meeting and How it Works.* Chicago: The University of Chicago Press, 2004.
  An analysis of over three decades of research of some 1,500 Vermont town meetings.
- **Bryan, Frank and John McClaughry.** *The Vermont Papers: Recreating Democracy on a Human Scale.* Chelsea, Vermont: The Chelsea Green Press, 1989.
  An original and provocative analysis of the relationship between democracy and community in Vermont and what can be done to preserve both.
- **Clark, Delia and Steven Glazer.** *Questing: A Guide to Creating Community Treasure Hunts.* Hanover, NH: University Press of New England, 2004.
  If you'd like to build interest in natural, historical, architectural, or other community "treasures," this manual will both inspire you and tell you how to do it.
- **de Tocqueville, Alexis.** *Democracy in America.* Cambridge: Sever and Francis, 1862.
  Still the most important book ever written about American democracy.
- **Lappé, Frances Moore, and Paul Martin DuBois.** *The Quickening of America: Rebuilding Our Nation, Remaking Our Lives.* San Francisco, CA: Jossey-Bass, 1994.
  A lively, workbook-style approach to improving participation in every citizen's "public life." Great tool for discussion groups.
- **Mansbridge, Jane.** *Beyond Adversary Democracy.* New York: Basic Books, 1980.
  A classic and ground-breaking treatment of face-to-face democracy, which includes the best treatment of town meeting in a single town in existence.
- **Putnam, Robert D.** *Bowling Alone: The Collapse and Revival of American Community.* New York: Simon and Schuster, 2000.
  An in-depth exploration of the decline of social capital and civic engagement in the United States.
- **Putnam, Robert D., and Lewis M. Feldstein.** *Better Together: Restoring the American Community.* New York: Simon & Schuster, 2003.
  Offers a dozen case studies from across America of building social capital.
- **Rice, Tom W., and Alexander F. Sumberg,** "Civic Culture and Government Performance in the American States," *Publius: The Journal of Federalism* 27 (Winter 1997); 114.
  Among the studies that rank Vermont first in civic culture.
- **Zimmerman, Joseph F.** *The New England Town Meeting.* Westport, Connecticut: Praeger Publishers, 1999.
  A comparative analysis of the legal structure of town meeting in the six New England states.
- **Zuckerman, Michael.** *Peaceable Kingdoms.* New York: Random House, 1970.
  Accepted as the most influential treatment of democracy and community in early New England.

About the authors

Susan Clark is an educator and facilitator, focusing on community sustainability and civic participation. She is an adjunct faculty member at Woodbury College, teaching community development. Susan's work with rural Vermonters strengthening communities has included directing a community activists' network, facilitating town visioning forums, and coordinating a rural grants program. An editor, writer, and advocate of public dialogue, she is a regular radio commentator and talk show co-host. A Vermont native, Susan lives with her family in Middlesex.

Frank M. Bryan is a professor of political science at the University of Vermont, and a well-known public speaker on Vermont life and politics. He is the author, coauthor, or editor of twelve books, including *Real Democracy: The New England Town Meeting and How It Works*; *The Vermont Papers: Recreating Democracy on a Human Scale*; and *Yankee Politics in Rural Vermont*, as well as several books of Yankee humor such as the bestseller *Real Vermonters Don't Milk Goats*. He grew up in Newbury, Vermont, and now lives in Starksboro.

The original illustrations in this book were provided by **Betsy Brigham**. She has done botanical and other illustrations for *Yankee Magazine*, *Wild Earth Journal*, the Green Mountain Club, The Nature Conservancy, the Vermont Heritage Program, and others. An artist and educator, Betsy lives with her family in Marshfield.

The photographs that appear on the cover were taken at town meetings across Vermont by **Jeb Wallace-Brodeur**. He is the chief photographer for *The Times Argus*, design and photo editor for the *Vermont Sunday Magazine*, and a contributing photographer for *Seven Days*. His photos have appeared in *Vermont Life*, *Vermont Magazine*, *The New York Times*, *The Boston Globe*, and numerous other publications. He lives in Montpelier.